Y0-BQZ-279

Love Gone Viral

Couples Who Make You Wanna Puke, And How To Be Part Of One

Pamela Fagan Hutchins

Love Gone Viral. Copyright © 2012 by Pamela Fagan Hutchins. All rights reserved. Printed in the United States of America. No part of this book may be used or reproduced in any manner whatsoever without written permission except in the case of brief quotations embodied in critical articles and reviews. For information, address SkipJack Publishing, P.O.B. 31160 Houston, TX 77231.

SkipJack Publishing books may be purchased for educational, business, or sales promotional use. For information, please write: Sales, SkipJack Publishing, P.O.B. 31160 Houston, TX 77231.

First U.S. Edition
Hutchins, Pamela Fagan
Love Gone Viral /by Pamela Fagan Hutchins
ISBN-13: 978-0-9882348-4-0 (SkipJack Publishing)

For my *last* husband:
Gypsy knight
Olive-skinned poet hero
Wild-haired surfer
Terrorizer of email
Musician, boss, misspeller
Father, coach, athlete
Lover mine

Acknowledgments

Huge thanks to my editor Meghan Pinson, who managed to keep my ego intact without sacrificing her editorial integrity. Thanks of generous proportions to my writing group, without whose encouragement and critiques I would not be publishing this book. Thanks to the power of infinity to my husband Eric, without whom I could make no one puke, and would feel pretty punky to boot.

Last but not least, thanks go to Alex Dumetriscu and Heidi for the great cover art. The photography credits go to Eric and me.

Other Books by the Author

The Clark Kent Chronicles: A Mother's Tale Of Life With Her ADHD/Asperger's Son, SkipJack Publishing

Hot Flashes And Half Ironmans: Middle-Aged Endurance Athletics Meets the Hormonally Challenged, SkipJack Pub.

How To Screw Up Your Kids: Blended Families, Blendered Style, SkipJack Publishing

Puppalicious And Beyond: Life Outside The Center Of The Universe, SkipJack Publishing

Saving Grace, SkipJack Publishing

Easy To Love, But Hard To Raise (anthology), DRT Press, edited by Kay Marner & Adrienne Ehlert Bashista

Easy To Love, But Hard To Teach (anthology), DRT Press, edited by Kay Marner & Adrienne Ehlert Bashista

Ghosts! (anthology contributor), Aakenbaaken & Kent, edited by Lynne Gregg & Julian Kindred

Prevent Workplace Harassment, Prentice Hall, with the Employment Practices Solutions attorneys

Table of Contents

Bring me a bucket.

When people tell me and my husband that we make them want to puke, we gaze into each other's eyes and say, "Thank you!" Then we go home and make sweet, sweet love, while singing each other Marvin Gaye songs and weaving promise rings out of sea grass and clover.

It's hard work, being this nauseating. The effort involved in all this damn smiling—you wouldn't want to take it on, I promise. Totally exhausting. Add to this burden our perfect children and our perfect careers, and you've got the makings of chronic fatigue syndrome, at least.

As my youngest daughter would say, "Whatever."

The first time an acquaintance told me, "Y'all are just so cute together it makes me want to puke," I wasn't sure how to take it. It sounded like a compliment, but it felt like a barb. I thought about her sterile marriage to a nice but unaffectionate man who didn't seem to find her interesting, and about how she laughed about him behind his back. I analyzed the green look in her brown eyes; I'd seen it in other people's eyes when I was with my husband. I concluded that, given the choice, I'd like to keep my relationship over hers, thank you very much. Also, while she seemed envious in a grudgingly admiring way, I'd never seen evidence that she worked to improve her own marriage. Not once. Did she think pukeworthiness just happened by accident, by a sprinkling of pixie dust? I don't believe it does.

So, yep, I am the lucky princess with the fairytale marriage. But I'm willing to bet even Cinderella and Prince Charming had their issues. Unfortunately for my prince, I habitually and publicly confess my more interesting failings, which inevitably involve our relationship from time to time. I guess that in addition to being half of a couple who makes you want to puke, I have diarrhea of the mouth (and fingers), too. Totally irresistible, I know.

I wish I could make it sound more scintillating than it really is, maybe write about how Eric is a compulsive gambler and I am a gender-reassignment success story, and the neighbors have called the cops to break up our fights on three separate occasions. That would be exciting, but it wouldn't be true.

The truth is boring. The truth is that we are as flawed as the next couple. I adore my almost-perfect husband, who puts up with me writing about him and being a gigantic pain in the ass. I love my normal, fallible kids and stepkids[1]. I love our messed-up, wacky life. But just because we adore and love each other, it doesn't mean the rest comes easily.

While I have no scandalous revelations for you, I can share the secrets of how two highly emotional, self-absorbed, over-committed Type-A losers at marriage (we are both each other's second spouse) manage our relationship into the true thing of beauty that it is.

And I do mean manage.

(Are you choking on that vomit yet? Stick around.)

If my day job counts, I am a so-called expert in human relations. As a hybrid employment attorney/human resources professional and consultant, I get paid to help grownups manage their workplace

---

[1] I'll refer to family members, friends, and clients from time to time. Names have been changed to protect the innocent—which Eric and I are far from.

relationships. The HR principles I apply at work are, in theory, principles for humans anywhere—like humans in a marriage, even a second marriage like mine.

There's a good reason doctors don't usually treat family members: when it comes to our loved ones, our rational selves are replaced by emotional creatures. Things get personal. Things get messy. All the psychological training in the world couldn't guarantee that someone (and by someone I mean me) will play fair.

Physician, heal thyself. HR Consultant, you too.

So it is with some embarrassment, and hopefully a bit of humility, that I will share our foibles and our feats. We understand how wrong we each got it on our first ride on the marriage-go-round, and we believe that through painful trial and error, we've finally gotten a grip on the brass ring. We know the statistics: over 40% of first marriages end in divorce and up to 67% of second do, too. The big issues— emotional intimacy, mutual support, compatibility, respect, sex, and money[2]—get even trickier when you add stepparenting, alimony, child support, ex-

---

[2] And, these days, I'd have to say that technology, like social media and smartphones, makes these issues more immediate and drives up the intensity.

spouses, and the "It's easier to say 'I quit' the second time" phenomenon. But we're beating the odds, and we want you to, as well. And so we begin. Keep your Pepto-Bismol handy.

THERE'S NOTHING UNDER THE CANOE, HONEY.

This is how we roll.

My husband and I went on our honeymoon in Montana in June, which unbeknownst to us was still the dead of winter. (We hail from the Caribbean.) At

the time, we were training for a Half Ironman triathlon,training for a Half Ironman triathlon, so we
needed to find an upper-body strength and aerobic
substitute for swimming during our two weeks of
bliss. Without taking the weather into account, we'd
decided that canoeing or kayaking would suffice.

So off we traipsed from Houston to Montana,
where we stayed in an adorable bed-and-breakfast
near Yellowstone, which we picked because the
owner advertised healthy organic food. The beets,
quinoa, and cauliflower kugel we were served for
breakfast weren't exactly what we'd hoped for, but
we felt fantastic. And hungry. Very, very hungry.

Our "Surprise! We're vegetarian!" B&B sat near a
tundra lake. For those of you who have not seen a
tundra lake, imagine a beautiful lake in a mountain
clearing surrounded by tall evergreens. Picture deer
drinking from crystalline waters, hear the ducks
quacking greetings to each other as they cruise its
glassy surface. Smell the pine needles in the air, fresh
and earthy.

And then imagine the opposite.

A tundra lake is in the highlands, no doubt, but
the similarity stops there: no trees, no windbreak, no
calm surface, and no scenery. Instead, it's an ice-
chunk-filled, white-capped pit of black water extend-

ing straight down to hell, stuck smack dab in the middle of a rock-strewn wasteland. Other than that, it's terrific.

Maybe it was because we were newlyweds, but somehow Eric intuited that I would love nothing more than to canoe this lake in forty-degree weather and thirty-five-mph winds, wearing sixty-seven layers of movement-restricting, water-absorbent clothing. Maybe it was because we were newlyweds, but I somehow assumed that because he knew of my dark water phobia and hatred of the cold (anything below seventy degrees), I was in good hands. My new husband assured me this lake was perfect for tandem canoeing.

So . . . we drove across the barren terrain to the lake. Eric was bouncy. I was unable to make my mouth form words other than "You expect me to get in that @#$%&&*$* canoe on that @#$%&&*$* lake?"

I promise he is smarter than this will sound. And that I am just as bitchy as I will sound. In my family, we call my behavior being the bell cow, as in "She who wears the bell leads the herd — and takes no shit from other cows."

Eric answered, "Absolutely, honey. It'll be great. Here, help me get the canoe in the water. I'd take it off the car myself, but with that wind, whew, it's like a sail. Careful not to dump it over; it's reallllly cold in there. Not like that, love. Where are you going? Did I say something wrong?"

I responded by slamming the car door. Anger gave way to tears that pricked the corners of my eyes. I stewed in my thoughts. I knew I had to try to canoe. I couldn't quit before I started. We were training, and if I didn't do it, Eric wouldn't do it, and that wasn't fair of me.

I exited the car. Eric was dragging the canoe out of the water and trying to avoid looking like a red flag waving in front of me.

Super-rationally, I asked, "What are you doing?"

He said, "Well, I'm not going to make you do this."

"You're not making me. I'm scared. I hate this. I'll probably fall in and all you'll find is my frozen carcass next summer. But I'm going to do it."

My poor husband.

We paddled clockwise around the lake in the shallows, where the waves were lowest, and I fought for breath. I'm not sure if it was the constriction of all the clothing layers or actually hyperventilation, but either way, I panted like a three-hundred-pound marathoner. It would have scared off any animal life within five miles if you could have heard me over the wind. Suddenly, Eric shot me a wild-eyed look and started paddling furiously toward the center of the lake.

"You're going the wrong way!" I protested.

"I can't hear you," he shouted back.

"Turn around!"

"I can't turn around right now, I'm paddling."

"Eric Hutchins, turn the canoe back toward the shore!"

And as quickly as his mad dash for the deep had started, it stopped. He angled the canoe for the shoreline.

"What in the hell was that all about?" I asked.

"Nothing, love. I just needed to get my heart rate up."

I sensed the lie, but I couldn't prove it. My own heart raced as if I had been the one sprint-paddling. For once, though, I kept my mouth shut.

The waves grew higher. We paddled and paddled for what felt like hours, but made little forward progress against the wicked-cold wind.

"Eric, I really want out of the canoe."

"We're halfway. Hang in there."

"No. I want out right now. I'm scared. We're going to tip over. I can't breathe."

"How about we cut across the middle of lake and shave off some distance? That will get you to the shore faster."

"I WANT TO GO THE NEAREST SHORE RIGHT NOW AND GET OUT OF THE #%$&(&^%#@% CANOE."

Now I really had to get out, because it was the second time I'd called the canoe a bad name, and I knew it would be out to get me.

Eric paddled us to the shore without another word. I'm pretty sure he thought some, but he didn't say them. I got out, almost falling over into the water and turning myself into a giant super-absorbent Tampax. He turned the canoe back over the water and continued on without me. This wasn't how I'd pictured it going down, but I knew I had better let him a) work out and b) work *me* out of his system. Looking like the Michelin man, I trudged back around the lake to the car and beat him there by only half an hour.

By the time we'd loaded the canoe onto the top of our rental car and hopped in, we were well on our way back to our happy place. Yes, I know I don't deserve him. I don't question it; I just count my blessings.

That night we dined out—did I mention we were starving to death on broccoli and whole-wheat tabbouleh?—to celebrate our marriage. Eric had arranged for flowers to be delivered to our table before we got there. The aroma was scrumptious: cow, cooked cow! Yay! And, of course, the flowers. I looked at Eric's wind-chafed, sunburned face and almost melted from the heat of adoring him. Or maybe it was from the flame of the candle, which I was huddling over to stay warm. What was wrong with the people in this state? Somebody needed to buy Montana a giant heater. We held hands and traded swipes of Chapstick.

He interrupted my moment. "I have a confession to make. And I promise you are really going to think this is funny later."

Uh oh. "Spill it, baby."

"Remember when I paddled us toward the middle of the lake as hard as I could?"

"I'm trying to block the whole experience out of my mind."

"Yeah, well, let me tell you, sweetness, it was about ten times worse for me than you. But do you remember what you said about falling in, yadda yadda, frozen carcass next summer, blah blah?"

I didn't dignify this with an answer, but he didn't need one and continued without much of a pause. "Well, you were in front of me, breathing into your paper bag or whatever, when I looked down, straight down, into the eyes and nostrils of a giant, bloated, frozen, very dead, fully intact, floating ELK CARCASS."

"You're lying."

"I am not. It was so close to the surface that if you hadn't still had those tears in your eyes, there is no way you wouldn't have seen it. You could have touched its head with your hand without even getting your wrist wet."

"No, you did NOT take me out on a lake with giant frozen dead animals floating in it." A macabre version of Alphabits cereal popped into my mind.

"Yes, I did," he said, and he hummed a few bars of Queen's "We Are the Champions."

"Oh my God. If I had seen it right then, I would have come unhinged."

"More unhinged. I know. I was terrified you would capsize us and then you would quadruple freak out in the water bumping into that thing. I had to paddle for my life."

He was right. I let him enjoy his moment; I'm glad he confessed. But I will never canoe on a tundra lake with Eric again. Even if I got my courage up, he would never invite me.

Cinderella, eat your heart out.[3]

---

[3] There's video of the tundra lake and other parts of our Montana trip on my YouTube channel, The Land of Pamelot. Sorry, there is no video of the elk.

I'M NOT GOING TO BE THE ASSHOLE THIS TIME.

When Eric and I said "I do" in Cruz Bay, St. John, we were madly in love and promised forever. Believed in forever. We were confident in forever, because we were soulmates. This was true love, and we each knew we were The One for each other, even though I'd never believed in any of that romance mumbo jumbo stuff before. Eric converted me.

Still, this left a lot up to chance. Because what we did not believe was that true love conquers all. We had already proven ourselves love-killers before, me with my ex, he with his. In our experience, passion and romantic love are fragile. If you don't nurture them, if you dump poison on them, they die.

We needed to figure out how not to poison our relationship. We had to do better than just love each other. We had to love *smart*; we had to love with *determination.* We absitively posilutely had to own up to what destroyed our past relationships, and make some serious commitments to doing things better with each other. We had to figure out who was the asshole.

If you're convinced that your ex was the A-hole, you may believe your next marriage will have a much greater chance of success. But even though you won't be marrying the *same* A-hole the second time around, you will be bringing the same *you* along; and to your ex, *you* were the A-hole. Woopsie. And both of you are probably at least partially right.

Eric and I knew we were each at least one of the A-holes that ruined our first marriages. It was time to do things differently. What's the definition of insanity, after all, but doing things the same way and expecting a different outcome?

When we got together, we had a big advantage over other second-marriage couples: we had worked together for four years before we fell in love. As colleagues, sometimes-rivals, and frenemies, we had already given each other a taste of our worst traits in unguarded moments. I already knew Eric was an A-hole. {Just kidding, honey.} There was no second chance for a carefully orchestrated great first-date impression for us. I could guess which of his behaviors contributed to the demise of his first marriage, as he could for me. (Cough, sensitivity, cough cough.)

And it was from our discussions about our worst traits that the origins of our Relationship Operating Agreement arose. That and from our first dozen knock-down drag-out battles. I had some empathy for his ex-wife. He understood the pain of my first husband. But slowly we came up with an ROA, which is really just a plan by another name. And, damn, I love me a good plan.

I know what you're thinking: "Well, at least she didn't lie. I'm definitely going to hurl." Hold onto your buckets, friends. It's not as crazy as it sounds.

Pretend for a second that you married a touchy-feely HR consultant. Imagine that she has a penchant for things like mission, vision, and values statements. Consider her love for goal-setting and accountability. Some of you have already mentally drawn up your divorce papers.

Eric didn't, thank goodness. Instead, he hunkered down with a yellow pad and sharp Number 2 pencil and took notes while we talked. And we talked and talked and talked and talked and talked. Remember how your mom used to tell you your face would get stuck that way when you crossed or rolled your eyes? Eric's nearly did.

We talked about our priorities, our values, our goals, our needs, our fears, our flaws, and our deepest, darkest secrets. Think Toby Keith's "I Want To Talk About Me" song, and you've just about got it. Sometimes it hurt, especially when we talked about our kids. Co-parenting each other's children was definitely the touchiest subject and the hardest issue, day by day. So hard that I wrote a whole separate book on it, so I'll save that discussion for *How To Screw Up Your Kids.*

By the time we had our ROA in place—had owned our faults and opened up about our needs—we felt safe with each other. One of the best moments in our relationship came after I behaved, ahem, *badly* toward Eric. Badly, but not out of character or outside Eric's expectations. I rallied, I apologized, I recommitted to the shared values behind our ROA.

Eric's response? "I see all your colors, Pamela. I like some of them better than others, but I love all of you."

Our ROA paints a picture of our relationship in vivid and beautiful colors, like those in a rainbow, and more. There's no turd yellow or coal black in a rainbow, but not every day is rainbows and butterflies. We all display our bad colors sometimes, and our ROA acknowledges the ugly colors and provides a plan to get us back to the ones we like the best.

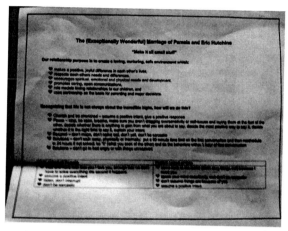

Note the crinkle in this paper. It doesn't just hang on a wall.

So here's how our ROA looks:

Our (Exceptionally Wonderful) Marriage
Mantra: Make it all small stuff.

Our relationship's purpose is to create a loving, nurturing, safe environment that enables us to

- Make a positive, joyful difference in each other's lives,
- Respect each other's needs and differences,

- Encourage each other's spiritual, emotional, and physical needs and development,
- Practice caring, open communication,
- Role-model loving relationships to our children, and
- Work as partners when we parent and make major decisions.

Because we recognize that life is not always about the incredible highs, we are committed to these strategies:

- Stop, breathe, and be calm.
- Allow ourselves to cherish and be cherished.
- Be positive. Assume a positive intent and give a positive response. Speak your mind as positively as possible.
- Be reasonable. Am I being oversensitive? Am I dragging my own issues in unnecessarily?
- Be considerate. Is there anything to gain from what I am about to say? Is this the right time to say it?
- Be respectful. Don't mope, don't name-call, don't yell, don't be sarcastic.

- Be open. Explain your intent.
- Be present. Don't walk away, physically or emotionally.
- Be aware of time and energy. After 60 minutes, stop talking. Schedule another conversation for 24 hours later if there's no resolution.
- Make it safe to cry "calf rope."
- Be it. Do the behaviors you're seeking in each other within an hour of the first conversation.
- Be loving. Don't go to bed angry or with things unresolved.

He asks of her:
- Trust and have faith that I love you, enough that we don't have to solve everything the second it happens.
- Assume a positive intent.
- Listen, don't interrupt.
- Don't be sarcastic.

She asks of him:
- Come back to me faster and don't drag things out, because I need you.

- Speak your mind assertively, and don't be sarcastic.
- Don't assume the actions I take are always because of you.
- Assume a positive intent.

We didn't get this smart on our own; both of us have had training on drafting these types of agreements in our work lives — one of us more than the other. I specialize in working with hyper-competitive, confident-bordering-on-egomaniacal executives who are wholly lacking in people skills, so I've spent years mediating, soothing, recalibrating, and at times walloping high-level business people into line. One of the best tools to get all the warring co-workers from different backgrounds to reach détente is an operating agreement. Even better? An operating agreement grounded in a shared mission, vision, and values. Ah, a lot like an ROA.

Now, I'm not churchy, but I'm very spiritual. And this is not a religious book, although I'll refer to my Christian faith at times. No matter your religion, I doubt you'll find anything in here that contradicts relationship advice you'd get from a faith-based book or counselor. This little book of mine makes a great supplement to whatever you are already doing. My experience and stories may help people, and for better or worse, I have almost no filter for personal disclosure.

Your ROA should center on the values you and your partner share. If God is your starting point, then put Him or Her there. If not, then put your other most important shared values at the heart of it, like honesty, integrity, or respect. You, as a couple, are 100% in control of the direction you take with this document. Everyone's ROA will look different, but feel free to poach mine all you want.

Our ROA is the compass to the true North of our relationship. When we misbehave, which we both do, but me more than Eric, we quickly navigate back to our shared commitments.

You're saying, "Commitment? Yeah, we've already got that—we are in a committed relationship."

I hear you, and sometimes I feel like I'm in a "committed" relationship, too, as in "Both of us are committed to the funny farm, because we keep looking for ways to pick each other apart." But we have found that taking the time to flesh out what we meant—*really* meant, in *detail* (Eric is a chemical engineer, after all)—when we promised to honor and cherish each other has made a huge difference in our marriage.

Do you both mean the same thing when you promise to respect each other? To me, respect is Eric listening to me. To Eric, respect is me shutting up. Those are not the same thing. Drafting the ROA made us intentionally reach an agreement on what our key concepts look like, feel like, and sound like, although we teach each other new interpretations now and then.

The most important concept we clarified? That it is our relationship we must focus on, not each of us as individuals. If we take care of the relationship and put it first, then we take care of each other. So, our every decision with regard to our relationship is about guarding, nurturing and protecting it. In other words, establishing and maintaining it is Job One. My top job is not Eric; his top job is not Pamela. Our top job is our wonderful relationship.

Sounds like work. Sometimes it is. But mostly it's fun, and it's worth it—nobody wants to be the A-hole twice.

How do pukey couples do it?

I can't speak for all couples, but Eric and I do it—the living-happily-ever-after part of love—very deliberately, as you may have guessed by now. We know we were meant to be together, and that our love for each other is an unexpected and precious gift. So we work hard to make sure we don't screw it up. We've both already been there and done that.

But the question I always get is *How*? How do couples like us make it work so well? Is it just that silly ROA? Well, no. No. It is much more—more fun, more effort, more joy, more tears—than the ROA: we have to *live* the ROA. What's more, we have to live the concepts and values that the ROA was built upon.

It's simple: See It. Say It. Honor It. Do It. Be It.

Some of you are wondering what "It" is, aren't you? Well, It is the relationship of your dreams. Try thinking of It this way: If you See your partner as the man of your dreams and your relationship as dreamy, Say things about him and It consistent with that vision, Honor him and what is important to him, Do dreamy relationship things for and with him, and then you just, by God, BE that dream partner for him by choosing the right attitude and right behavior to nurture that dream, then you will succeed in creating and sustaining It. Got it? Good.

See, wasn't it easier when I just said "It?"

But that's all. Really. If you want to see that in formulaic terms, which Eric the engineer does, it is: See + Say + Honor + Do + Be = It.

We *See* the good in our relationship, our future, and each other, because what you see is what you get. We look away from the dark side. How I choose to interpret the reason Eric makes a snappy comment, for example, can either be that it is a) about me and because he is a bad person, or b) about something else that will make perfect sense when he explains to me later. I wouldn't have married him if I believed he was a bad person, so why would I start assuming he is after I said "I do"?

We *Say It*. We leave notes for each other, and sometimes I look the other way when he goes over our budget buying me tulips. We send cards through the mail, surprise each other with dollar store gifts, we text, IM, Facebook, Twitter, and email our fingers off, and tell anyone that will listen how lucky we are. We connect any way we can, and we deliberately build each other and our relationship up.

We *Honor It* and respect that which is important to the other. I bicycle, run, and swim! He edits manuscripts and does the cha-cha! I put up with his obsession with the Arizona Cardinals. We play and sing like a really crappy old-age-home rock band. It works for us.

We take the time to date. At least once a month, we trade the honor of planning for and executing a date befitting how we feel about each other. We never do the same thing twice for our dates. We LOVE date night. We've done everything from neighborhood musicals and in-the-round plays to laser tag and karaoke.

Oh yeah, and we *Do It*. We hold hands in public and in private, we snuggle, and we, well, we enjoy each other in a private way. (I hope that's discreet enough for my grandmother and mother-in-law!)

And then there's *Be It*. When the love of my life pisses me off, I revisit what we see and I choose to be. I'm not going anywhere. He's not going anywhere. Whatever is wrong is just stuff, and can be dealt with. And so we can be what we see, we deal with the stuff. Immediately or very quickly, whichever comes first. Although we don't pretend love means saccharine sweetness 24/7, we do our best to close the door and talk outside our kids' earshot. Sometimes for hours. Sometimes calmly, holding hands; and sometimes less calmly, with Eric holding me at bay. We revisit our ROA, we regroup and recommit.

But we believe that it is all just stuff, and that we are each all in. The goal in our discussions is to make it as easy and beautiful as possible, not to prove one of us is right and the other is a jerk. We must protect It — The Relationship Of Our Dreams — so that it is just as strong and vibrant when we are ninety as it is now, when we are in our early twenties.[4]

-----

[4] We may look a bit older than that, but I assure you, I'm twenty-three. Just ask my seventeen-year-old son.

I'm going to spend the rest of this book fleshing out what I mean by all that seeing, saying, honoring, doing, and being stuff, sometimes by explaining and sometimes by telling stories. Because while true love is a gift, happily-ever-after doesn't happen by accident, friends. Claim your fairytale ending and make everyone around you just a little bit sick.

PART ONE: SEE IT

WHAT ARE YOU LOOKING FOR?

When people think I'm making all this stuff up about my story book marriage and they tell me to get real, it's a little frustrating. I'm not alone here; my friend Nan[5] knows what I'm talking about. She and her husband make people want to puke, too. She feels exactly as I do about this.

"I've ridden the drama train before," Nan wrote to me a while ago. "So has my husband. We are striving for peace. Our life is real and not without issues, but our marriage truly is wonderful. Part of why it is wonderful is that we always look for the best in each other, and we talk nice about each other."

---

[5] http://lbddiaries.com/blog

This resonates with me. And not just because I like Nan, who is an ordained minister, as well as a writer and a friend. It resonates with me as a human, and as someone who has made it her life's work to enter problematic workplace situations and help diagnose and fix problems between people. Through this, I have come to believe that if you look hard enough for something, you will find it. If you think people are out to get you, you'll find signs that they are. If you believe things aren't your fault, you'll see the culpability of others. If you think others are belittling you, you'll discover evidence of belittling attitudes.

But if you believe that others are heroic and awesome, you will find that as well.

Don't believe me? Try it. Just for today, make a list of all the things the most important person in your life does right. All of them. Big and small. Even the ones you take for granted. Look hard. Make that list a novel. Notice the things they do in all aspects of their life. Did he get up on time and make it in to work? Did she obey the law on the way? Did he let you know what his plans are for this evening? Did he kiss the kids goodbye on his way out the door? Did she call her mother? Put her plate in the sink? Smile at you? Remain married to you despite your many faults? Bring in the mail? Practice good hygiene? Not leave the cap off the toothpaste? I mean it. List them all.

Don't let yourself look for <u>any</u> negatives, not for a single second. Today is a day for gathering positive evidence. Reject critical interpretations. Banish thoughts about faults. Refuse to look for sins and omissions.

Nan reminded me that the Bible says to "Focus your thoughts on what is true, noble, righteous, pure, lovable or admirable, on some virtue or on something praiseworthy" (Philippians 4:8). I remember hearing a sermon on this verse when I was younger, but I interpreted it differently then than I do now. I thought I was supposed to surround myself with only virtuous people (not that I heeded that call), and I believed I was being told to strive for those traits — which I did sometimes, and other times not so much. I am looking at it with new eyes today, thanks to Nan.

What if we applied this teaching to how we think about others? Our spouses, sure, but even our co-workers, bosses, kids, friends, and neighbors? It's harder to find the goodness and light in some of them, but don't take the easy way out on this. Look harder.

What you look for, you will find. What you focus on is what you see. Your thoughts become your reality. I choose to fill my thoughts with positive interpretations of my husband and my others. Will you join me? What do you have to lose?

Here's the start of a list I made:

- ♥ Eric took Clark to school and texted me from work that he loved me.
- ♥ Clark got up the first time I asked him to.
- ♥ Susanne fed the animals without a reminder.
- ♥ Liz sent personal thank yous for all her Christmas gifts.

See how easy that was? Thanks, Nan. Now, everyone out there, it's your turn.

BEFORE NOW

Love makes us do crazy things. I am a writer of prose. (You can decide for yourself whether I am any good at it.) Whatever level of skill I have at writing prose, I have much less at writing poetry. Yet love brings out my desire to describe what I see in my husband and in our relationship in many forms, even in bad poems and songs.

Has someone you loved ever written you a goofy love letter or a terrible poem, or drawn you an unrecognizable picture? Have they made you a crazy video, knitted you some holey socks, or cooked you an inedible gourmet meal? You loved it, didn't you? It wasn't the quality, it was the fact that love for you moved the other person to the gesture. At the risk of receiving some incredibly bad reviews of this book, I'm sharing some of my poetic scribblings with you as we go along. If it inspires even one of you to take a chance in building a better relationship, my humiliation is worth it.

Each time you read one of my rhymey-rhymey chapters, ask yourself: How far would I go to show my partner what I see in her?

Without further ado, here is a poem by me, called "Before Now."

***

Before
Before was beige,
Flashes of tan,
Oatmeal-colored days
And nights of brown with brownest mornings
My thick muddy center the gray of day-old coffee

Now
Now is a kaleidoscope pointed at the sun
My eyes squeezed so tight, colors I can't count
light up my head, warm my cheeks from the inside
Your eyes glittery camouflage and heart peek-a-boo
red

Now is hue.

POLARITY

The discussion of love always turns my thoughts to polarity, maybe because my super-romantic husband is a chemical engineer. You'll remember from chemistry class that polarity is when atoms bond together because of their electrostatic attraction. Come on, y'all: covalent bonding? Ionic bonding? The whole "oppositely-charged ions" thing in chemical compounds? Totally romantic.

Polarity = electrostatic attraction. Just let those words slip over your lips a few times. Electrostatic attraction. Electrostatic attraction. E-lec-tro-static-attraction. Sexy words. Romantic words.

Basically, two atoms that aren't even aware of each other's existence cross paths in orbit. *Zing.* They pull a little closer together. They don't even need an introduction or a first date. They orbit closer. *Zing, zing.* Each time, uncontrollably, irresistibly, they come nearer. Finally, irrevocably, they bond. They literally share electrons; they become one. These two atoms might not even LIKE each other. Their bonding might really mess their shiz up in real life. Other atoms might not understand their attraction. But they have no choice; it is fate.

Sometimes, if the atoms are lucky, they do like each other. If they are really blessed, they might even love and adore each other and live happily ever after. And if so, they'd better appreciate it, because they could have ended up with an ionic bond to some alcoholic jackass with a compulsive gambling problem who lives with his mother, and refuses to shave his back hair. How bad would that suck?

But just imagine, when the universe gets it right . . . magic can happen. Maybe there is a fifteen-year-old male atom out there, growing up in the U.S. Virgin Islands, that sees in its dreams a blond-haired, blue-eyed, tightly-wound female atom who would do an Ironman and run marathons with him. Who moves from the islands to New Mexico, where that girl's family has bought a home three hours away. Who, one year later, walks the same sidelines at Texas Tech University's football stadium one month before her. Who moves to Dallas, where he and the girl work in buildings next to each other. Who attends a New Year's Eve celebration in 2000, sitting one table away from her. Closer, closer.

Maybe there's a fifteen-year-old female atom out there, two thousand miles away, that sees in her dreams a dark-eyed, wild-haired, lanky male atom who would talk her into an Ironman and run marathons with her. Who moves to the islands from Texas, driven by an inner force she can't rationalize. Who meets an overly intense male co-worker that she doesn't really like at first. Who sits three feet across a table from him and feels a magnetic pull that terrifies her. That looks into his eyes and in a flash recognizes the boy from her dreams and sees the same recognition cross his face before he shuts it down. Closer, closer.

A million orbits have passed since their dreams. Life went on. Fission resulted in the production of small atoms, five special, small atoms. But still, this moment came, inevitably.

Maybe the dreamers are the same two that hold hands and bind forever in a wind-swept gazebo overlooking Cruz Bay five years and a thousand storms after their eyes first meet. That whisper about polarity, nose-to-nose while three teenagers are up later than they are supposed to be, thinking the two don't know they've all sneaked back onto Facebook after bedtime.

See what I mean? Chemistry = romance.

And so, I write to celebrate the force that polarity exerts on my life, and to thank Eric for sharing his ~~geeky~~ scientific view of our love, and having the patience to explain the concept to me over and over until I kinda sorta almost understand it.

KEEPING IT IN FOCUS

Seeing the good in each other isn't always easy; sometimes I get distracted by all the other stuff. In order to focus on the truth of Eric's best traits, I have to remove the distractions. The emotional distractions. The detractors from emotional intimacy.

Maybe you are part of a couple comprised of two perfect people who never let their emotions get the best of them. We aren't. I venture into irrationality when I PMS, which Eric says is a permanent condition for me. Eric's brain short-circuits when his powerful emotions overload his system. We decided at one point that we needed help.

To that end, we purchased two books. Our goal was to rely on a book with both text and exercises to improve our already wonderful yet all-too-real relationship by giving us a structured way to address our challenge areas. (And anyone married to me will be knee-deep in challenge areas.) *The Complete Idiot's Guide to Intimacy* was our first purchase. We didn't want to overestimate our capabilities.

When our daughters found this book on our bedside table, they got the giggles. "Oh my God, you bought a book about S-E-X? Hehehehehehehe."

"No, dearies. We bought a book about I-N-T-I-M-A-C-Y."

If you are older than a teenager and think intimacy is only about sex, then you really do need this book. Intimacy includes physical touch, which can include sex. But intimacy is much, much more. Intimacy starts at the emotional level. It's trust, shared secrets, and respect. To understand what this means, approach it from this perspective: Think about what fidelity means to you, with your partner. Chances are that an emotional betrayal—like an online confidante—would damage your relationship as much or more than a physical betrayal, because it replicates (or replaces) the core of the intimacy you promised only to each other. Or maybe the damage to your emotional intimacy comes through a lack of respect, like speaking destructively to or about each other.

Eric and I spent a few months reading aloud, discussing, and completing the exercises from the *Idiot's Guide* together. Every night. No matter what. And some nights we were sleepy and finished in the wee hours. But we stuck to it, because The Relationship comes first.

One of the exercises that benefitted us greatly was writing out strategies to defuse our most volatile issues. You know, the ones that come up over and over, each time with a nuclear explosion, leaving the two of you looking past each other with the thousand-yard stare, like money or communication. {Oops, am I airing *my* issues here? Bad me!}

It is not wise to write about how you are going to deal with your partner's thin skin and irrational beliefs, and then show your notebook to him, so we didn't share our exercises with each other. We wrote out our strategies in personal exercises, but we used them, and we found that they work. Because they are all about how I will be accountable for nurturing the intimacy of The Relationship, not how he will treat me. If I can focus on myself, and keep intact the way I view Eric, we both come out stronger for it.

Who knew we were so smart at this relationship thing?

We often pull these strategies back out and re-read them to ourselves. It helps me focus; it determines not only how I behave, but what I see. If my goal is to protect The Relationship, then I won't enter a high-risk situation without revisiting my plan of action. I did this recently when Eric and I tackled one of our most volatile subjects: co-parenting stepkids, and what is and is not fair. I think I handled the situation far better, as a result.

Rather than share my personal strategy on co-parenting (why show the kids my cards, after all), I'll share one of my seven "hot button" strategies:

***

My Responsibilities for Positive Reframing and Solutions

1. When Eric feels like I purposefully fail to misunderstand him:

<u>My problem</u>: It frustrates him when others, especially me, do not understand him. He believes he is clear – in his mind, he is clear. Often the topic carries emotional baggage for him, so it is important to him to be understood. When I don't understand him, he is frustrated. It makes him feel inadequate, difficult, disconnected and unheard. It can become a huge issue of self-esteem.

<u>What I need to do about it</u>:
•Do not get emotional – expect this to be hard for him.
•Make it OK, not awkward or tense. Stay calm, be kind and patient, touch him.
•Seek to clarify my understanding, say what I do understand. Tell him I want to understand.
•In the end, even if I do not completely understand, say what I do understand as fully, honestly, and lovingly as possible.
•Make sure I use the right tone and facial expressions to match my message.

***

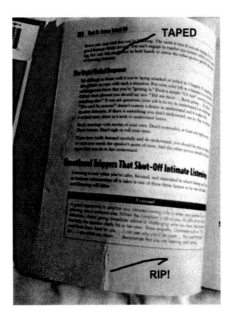

Lest you think that we skipped along the path picking daisies and singing tra-la-la while we did these exercises, please note the picture, above, of page 150. This section of the book is titled "Emotional Triggers that Shut-Off Intimate Listening." See the big piece of Scotch tape? That's what happens when one person sticks a hot poker into the other person's eye, or when the book prompts a conversation that doesn't go very well. One of us may or may not have held the book lovingly in front of the other person's face to show them up close and personal exactly the part they were doing wrong.

For that matter, see the picture at the beginning of this chapter, with the cover of the book? The book lost its back cover in that same interaction, when it may or may not have been lofted gently in the air in the general direction of one's beloved. (It was totally Eric's fault, not mine.)

The other book we bought was *365 Questions for Couples*[6]. The premise of this book is that you must never quit talking to and learning about each other, to really see the whole person that is your partner. Once we finished *An Idiot's Guide*, we started reading three or four of these questions per night and taking turns going first to give our answer. We loved it when we knew each other's answer. We loved it even more when we shocked each other with new thoughts and ideas. We've seen areas of commonality that we didn't expect, and areas of Grand Canyon divide that surprised us. And we dealt with the gulfs right then, instead of finding out about them in the middle of a crisis, twelve years from now.

I'm lucky—I'm married to a man that didn't groan and roll over when I asked him to explore ways to protect our emotional intimacy and The Relationship. If your partner is less than enthusiastic

---

[6] By Dr. Michael J. Beck, et al.

about this kind of approach and work, don't let that stop you from tackling it on your own. By making tiny changes in your own behavior, you may create shock waves of changes in him or her. Even if you don't, take a look in the mirror. If the person you see staring back at you is not perfect, then what do you have to lose by working on your own shit?

And, yes. I'm always this annoying.

DOLLAH DOLLAH BILL Y'ALL

Let's start with a little quiz and expand on some points I've only touched on briefly. First question: Do you know what the number one cause of divorce is? Second question: Is the leading cause of divorce different in second marriages?

Many people believe money, across the board, is the leading cause of divorce, which is a conception left over from many, many decades ago. But almost every study I've read ranks incompatibility, lack of emotional support, sexual problems, and domestic abuse higher than money problems[7] in the demise of

---

[7] Money isn't the culprit in most divorces. Liz Pulliam Weston.
http://articles.moneycentral.msn.com/CollegeAndFami

first marriages. Finances usually make the top five, though, and they complicate the situation when the other risk factors are present. If you are incompatible with your spouse, is it partly because you are financially incompatible? If you feel emotionally unsupported, is it because you and your partner are not financially aligned?

Second marriages fail at an even higher rate than first marriages, usually because of stepparenting conflicts. But money is still in the top five. Consider the impact of child support and alimony on the already challenging subject of finances[8], and wham bam, you've got yourself a burlap bag of rattlesnakes.

The biggest factor in marital success, especially the second time around (or if you're a particularly slow learner, the third or so on), is understanding why your previous relationship(s) failed, and how your traits and behaviors contributed to the failure. If you and your partner develop an ROA or some other mechanism, you can get clear — really, really clear —

---

ly/SuddenlySingle/MoneyIsntTheCulpritInMostDivorces.aspx

[8] Second marriage can be as difficult as the first one. Anne Kass.
http://www.alllaw.com/articles/family/divorce/article49.asp

on what your own issues and hot buttons are, and plan to act differently and handle them better this time.

For me, money is a major hot button. It can distract me from keeping my outlook rosy, and potentially from focusing on my husband through a positive lens. Don't get me wrong—many other factors contributed to the failure of my first marriage, and by the time you finish reading this book, I'll bet you'll have ferreted them all out for yourself. Money just happens to be an emotional area for me.

My parents raised me to be conservative, especially concerning fiscal matters. My father is so tight that my brother Bruce says you can't retrieve a penny clinched in his . . . fist (actually, he says "cheeks"). Growing up, Mom made Bruce and me promise never to tell our father how much blue jeans really cost. My Uncle Jack wrote Dad a thank you note after my first wedding, stressing just how many premium liquor drinks he had ordered from the bar on my father's tab, and mentioning the total bill a time or three for good measure. Dad is not just tight; Dad is tight, opinionated, and has a will of iron. It's a lethal combination.

Growing up in the image of my father, I learned to save money. Even more, I learned not to spend it in the first place. I learned the difference between want and need. I learned that I was expected to hold a job. At my parents' insistence, I lied about my age when I was fifteen to get a job at McDonald's. {I'm sorry, McDonald's.} They explained that it was a stupid law and kids my age should be working any time they could. I wore a hairnet. I'm still scarred.

At Texas A&M, I drove my roommate Jenny crazy by refusing to run my car's air conditioner in the humidity and heat of a College Station, Texas, summer. I waited tables at a nice Italian restaurant, and the owner allowed us to eat all the salad and bread we wanted. And, people, I am here to tell you, I gorged myself. If I stuffed myself at the beginning and end of each shift, it eliminated two meals I would have otherwise had to pay for. My family allowed me to keep some of the money I made, but the lion's share went to defer the cost of my schooling above my scholarships. I had friends living on student loans plus their meager earnings, so I counted myself very lucky to have parents who were willing and able to cover the bulk of my expenses in undergraduate and law school.

I don't mean to say I didn't live a privileged life. I did. I do. But I can do more with one dollar than most people can do with $100. I buy generic. I use coupons. I wait for sales. I work—hard. As hard as I used to play! And almost as hard as my husband. When one of our kids needs something (not wants—*needs*), Eric and I will make it happen.

It's not that difficult for me, thanks in large part to my upbringing. It just requires willpower and deferring or eliminating self-gratification. {There may be a reason some of my friends and family call me "the General."} Decide what you have available to spend, prioritize your needs, and spend only what you have. Maybe your house will have to be smaller than you want, or you will live in an apartment or a trailer. It may not be what you dreamed of, but no one guaranteed our every desire a birthright. In fact, as my warm, soft, and fuzzy padre often told me, "No one said life would be easy, or even fun." Damn straight.

Yep, life isn't easy. We all face some tough stuff. For some of us, the tough stuff is medical, for others, like me, it's struggles with hormones and moods, alcohol (stay tuned), and a failed first marriage. And some, like my husband, have battled financial woes and bankruptcy.

Did you catch that? Ultra-fiscally-responsible Pamela married the man of her dreams and knowingly stepped into his impending bankruptcy for a failed business. Out of the frying pan and into the leaping flames of a bonfire I jumped. I wouldn't have had it any other way, because we are partners and this is love. But some people close to me questioned my sanity.

Before we married, Eric and I spent a considerable amount of time and energy on our financial strategy and responsibilities. It took a lot to get me to my comfort zone. And even though I abhorred the thought, we entered a prenuptial agreement that kept his bankruptcy away from my assets.

I worked incredible hours so we could make our household's ends meet with my two and one of his kids living with us, and one of his in college. He used nearly his entire salary to pay alimony to his married, nonworking ex-wife, and to repay his parents for personal loans that propped up the failing business he and his ex-wife had shared.

Today, Eric is a changed man. He follows my detailed budget and listens to me explain the monthly cash flow, positive and negative deltas, and discovered opportunities for spending reductions. He swears I wait for PMS to hit before I update my spreadsheets. And he's right; why not combine the two and get all the pain over with at once?

It probably doesn't sound like a fairy tale. Yet it is, because we were honest and open with each other about the situation and our feelings about it. We made a plan, and we lived the plan. Sure, it was hard. Harder on him than me, because he hated bringing what he viewed as his biggest failure into my life. But consider the positive for a moment: the incredible emotional intimacy we built by our respectful discussions and partnership about our finances. Imagine the unconditional acceptance he felt that I loved *him*, not his (nonexistent) bank account. Picture how clearly we saw each other, and how we were able to focus on each other's positive traits by eliminating ugly surprises and financial uncertainty.

As a result of marrying Eric, I learned how it felt to walk on the other side of the line, to live in a household where we had no prayer of earning enough to break even. And over a few years, we found ways to make more money and eliminate more expenses, and we dug our way out of that incredible hole. The financial part of our relationship is not fun. Truth: There are days I resent the living hell out of giving away what I work to earn to pay for the sins of a past life I didn't live. *Sigh, deep breath.*

Every day, though, I feel blessed to be with the love of my life, and grateful beyond anything I can express that he confessed upfront and left behind the spending habits of his past life. Honesty and partnership: I couldn't ask for more.

ROCK FLOWERS

Eric and I commemorate our trips with a memory touchstone, something local and usually quirky. It started when we bought a jeweled wire gecko the day before our wedding, continued with a carved grizzly on our honeymoon, and kept going with our anniversary mementos, including a wooden armadillo, a metal cowboy, and painted trumpeting frogs. All are displayed proudly in our family room.

One anniversary, we happened upon a farmer's market in Montgomery, Texas, north of Houston. I begged him not to make me go, fearing we would casually spend money on useless junk.

"Just for a minute," he cajoled.

I caved. We entered. I sprinted ahead, as I am wont to do. The first booth I came upon featured baked goods made by a little old lady and her granddaughter. Before Eric even caught up to me, I'd shelled out $4.00 for homemade chocolate chip cookies.

"I thought you told me not to let you eat any more sugar this weekend?" he asked.

I shot him a look, and he wised up. These were consumables; how could that be a waste of money?

The next booth held soap and body products, and it was run by a wonderful father of seven who made the products himself with his wife. Maybe I didn't need all these specialty soaps, but we could use them as gifts, so I bought a bag full.

"But you . . ." Eric started to say, then trailed off into a smile.

Meanwhile, the wind had picked up to just below tornado level, so the vendors were packing up their booths. All except two young men with a display of rocks. They didn't need to escape the wind; the rocks weren't going anywhere.

The men were brothers, brothers with long beards and earnest green eyes. They called their creations "rock flowers," and made them by banding ten local stones together as petals with copper wire.

"We're going to make some rock wreaths once our welding skills improve," one of them said, holding up a sample wreath, made pre-improvement.

I hid my shudder, but it was as much with delight at the perfection of the moment as anything. Eric and I huddled, the same idea in our heads. Rock flowers. It was meant to be. Eric turned to the brothers. "How much for that one?"

"We'd like $100 for it and the display stand [a large flat-surfaced rock]. Or $30 for the flower. Or if that's too much, we'd give it to you for $25."

So we carried off our $30 (of course!) rock flower, eating our cookies and breathing in the fragrance of our new soaps.

"You realize you just authorized expenditure of $30 on ten rocks out of their backyard," Eric said.

I pretended I didn't hear him and took another bite of my cookie.

IF A TREE FALLS IN THE FOREST

My beloved accuses me of bending the truth at times. I'll admit, occasionally I take poetic license to make things more, um, compelling. But I start with the truth in what I see.

Lately, the truth was that our tranquil weekends at our property in Nowheresville, Texas—the planned site of our someday-after-childrearing home—had become even more idyllic. [This is a literary example of irony. In real life, irony is known as sarcasm.] That's because we had added manual labor to Eric's normal slacker agenda for triathlon training in extreme Texas summer heat. Our manual labor was for a good cause: my parents had lent us their skid loader, and we were using it to clear our driveway and home site. And to build a running trail for Ironman training.

We'd tried this skid loader/tractor exercise before, when the pond was low in the winter, to clear out debris and prep it for spring rains. It cost $1,000 for one day, including repairs to the damaged skid loader. [Don't ask.] It was after this day of skid-loadering that we ended up, six months of Texas drought later, with a dry pond that looked like a Jack and the Beanstalk weed pit—a pond that used to contain actual water, lily pads, frogs, and a bazillion different kinds of birds. Where I come from, we called things like this "pouring money down a dry hole."

To augment our current tree / bramble / brush / bush / land-clearing capabilities, Eric invested $700 in a new industrial chainsaw and a gas-powered pole saw. We'd tried the chainsaw exercise before, too. It cost $250, and the unit was deemed unworthy of repair after its time in the hands of Bubba-mon, aka Eric, our island boy turned Texan.

Where was I? Oh yes, our visit to Lowe's for deforestation equipment. Bubba-mon presented me with dust masks, gloves, and safety glasses, all of which I wore, and none of which did he let touch his skin the entire weekend. We loaded up the dogs and two of our teenagers, and we headed to Nowheresville.

Our last two visits to Nowheresville for the purpose of skid-loadering had not gone so well. On the second-to-last visit, someone forgot the keys to the Quacker, the secondhand travel trailer that we'll call home out there until we build our house. On the last visit, someone forgot the keys to the skid loader. Someone is really a dumbass. Yes, Someone's name is Pamela. Anyway, this time we were ready, with color-coded, tagged sets of keys in triplicate.

Susanne set the tone immediately. Here is a picture of her, five minutes into the weekend. Check out the look on her precious, precious face. I can't tell for sure, but I think she's smiling at her stepfather.

Don't let her expert grip on the pole saw fool you; she didn't actually use that thing.

Here is a picture of her the next day, after we sent her non-working butt back to Houston, where she spent the night with a friend dolling up and taking pictures. At least she didn't go anywhere looking like that. We think/hope. Susanne 1, parents 0.

On day one, I started using the pole saw and Bubba-mon headed to the shed to fire up the skid loader, which roared like a champ. But that's all it did. The bucket boom would not lift, and as he backed it up, the bucket wedged three yards of sand underneath the belly of the machine, causing it to turtle with all four wheels spinning helplessly in the middle of a mighty sandstorm. After only one and a half hours of jacking its eight tons up on a car jack rated for two tons, and then shoving cedar logs under the wheels and digging sand out from under the belly, we had it free. Free, and still broken and unusable.

The purpose of our trip, remember, was to use the skid loader. And we had a whole three-day weekend to do it in, except now we had no skid loader. All righty then.

We gave each other a quick smooch and reminded ourselves how lucky we were to be together, and Bubba-mon fired up the big saw. He instructed me to stay clear so I wouldn't get hit by debris. No problem.

For a while, we got a fair amount of clearing done. Bubba-mon chainsawed and I dragged the branches into a giant pile. The temperature peaked at a hundred degrees, ten degrees cooler than the previous weekend. I was feeling pretty good about life, when all of a sudden, something large, hard, and heavy crunched into the top of my head.

Holy shit. It was a tree. My enthusiastic husband had decided to test his chainsaw on some slightly bigger subjects, and my head was the recipient of his successfully severed branch.

No one else witnessed the event. My son Clark reacted to my news that Eric's tree had almost paralyzed me with "What were you doing standing in the way, Mom?"

Grrrr. This was almost funny, considering the source, Clark the ADHD "Huh? What?" WonderKid.

Bubba-mon himself choked out an apology and then said, "I've got enough on my hands worrying about my own safety without having to worry about yours, too."

The man had a point, even if his comment was not well-advised fifteen short seconds after my brush with death. He was dripping blood from multiple unbandaged wounds already. Lucky he's so cute and buys me tulips on Fridays. What he should have bought me, though, was a hard hat.

Rarer than Sasquatch, we call this sighting "Teenager Briefly At Worksquatch."

Eric said, "You're going to write about this like it was a giant redwood."

"Texas doesn't have redwoods. That's California," I said. "And the tree had a three-and-a-half-inch trunk."

"All that hit you were a few leaves," he said.

Maybe it wasn't quite this big.

I pointed to the knot on my head. "Wanna feel what the leaves did?"

He shook his head and tried again. "I did tell you to stand back."

"Only with you would thirty-five feet be insufficient, given the task."

He relented and wrapped me in a sweaty hug. "Maybe it wasn't a redwood, but it was big enough that I really worried that I'd hurt you. I'm sorry."

I had already forgiven him, though, because (and now this really is the 100% truth) I should have known to stay a half-mile away from my husband while he operated an industrial cutting implement.

That night, the air conditioner in the Quacker shut off at two a.m., a nightmare only Bubba-mon could have predicted, knowing as he did that we didn't have enough gas in the generator to last the night. It had run out at 2:00 a.m., when the temperature inside rose to meet the pleasant outdoor temperature of eighty-seven degrees. Bad Bubba-mon. All I really wanted after that hot night with a sore head was a cold drink, but, shockingly, Clark had left the cooler open. I settled for a warm Sobe.

Clark and I had counted on being on the road back to Houston with a Suburban full of mangled machinery early in the morning, but Bubba-mon had other plans. We all worked diligently until Bubba-mon had finally broken both the chainsaw and the pole saw. Clark and I were dying of exhaustion and couldn't believe it had taken him so long, but we were relieved that we could finally head home. To our horror, Bubba-mon whipped out the clippers and machete. Clark and I rebelled, and Eric put them away after only fifteen minutes of solo chopping.

As we got ready to drive away, Bubba-mon—completely forgetting for a moment the skid-loader dig-out that had started our work weekend—said, "Let's try out the new driveway," and pointed the Suburban into the partially cleared forest.

I didn't even have time to yell, "Sand!!!!!!!!!" much less, "Honey, don't you think the Suburban might get stuck in all that dry sand? Why don't we wait and try it once we lay the gravel?"

Day two ended much like day one began, with a massive dig-out project. But no one went to the emergency room, and really, what other criteria do you need to judge a weekend in Nowheresville by? We aren't going to let something little like a giant redwood to the head come between us and our someday home together.

WAS SHE A BAD PICKER
OR A BAD PARTNER?

I grew up listening to Captain & Tennille spin their songs of love, some of them foot-stomping fun—"You Better Shop Around" (yeah, baby) or "Love Will Keep Us Together"—and others touching the deepest part of my young soul—"Muskrat Love," anyone? One song in particular stuck with me, though: "The Wedding Song." Take a moment to Google the lyrics, and keep them open for reference. I'd put them here, but then I'd have to pay the songwriters. You guys know how cheap I am, so get to Googling.

It's the memory of these lyrics that sent me into a tidal wave of emotion at a wedding I attended, the wedding of a couple that deserves membership in the vomit-inducing club, for sure. I want to tell you the bride's story, a story of hope for many of us, a story that will sound and feel oh-so-familiar, and a story of second — and third — chances.

Once upon a time, a beautiful, exotic woman gave up on love. Love, and the absence of love, had kicked the crap out of her for a decade, so she spent the next ten years with her chin lifted high. She showed the world that she didn't need love, she didn't need any One. She mothered her two children and became a great success at everything but love. When men would woo, she had only to look into the mirror at the scars no one could see and look deep into those big brown eyes to find her no. Was she a bad picker or a bad partner? Who knew? Who cared. All that mattered was not going through the pain again for something she, a strong woman, didn't need, for something that she really didn't believe existed anymore.

And then she met a man. A man who wanted to marry her. And she had to look in that mirror again and ask her twice-divorced self: What's to be the reason for us to become man and wife?

Not security. Not money. Not the promise of children. Not family pressure or religious convictions. For God's sake, they could just live together after all, keep it simple, make the split less painful (or at least less costly) when it came. It had always come before.

But she said yes. Because it had happened: that blinding flash of hope so exquisitely true she couldn't tell if it was pleasure or pain.

Loving is the answer. Real love. The kind of love only romantics — strong people — believe in. She believes in something she has never, not in all her forty-four years, seen before.

Oh, there *is* love.

Yes, there is *love* . . .

And, so, on a lovely day in March, this dear, dear, beautiful, wounded woman lifted high her chin once again, but this time also her heart, and announced to the world that she took this man, not just as Someone, but as The One. She and her new husband stood with their lightning in a bottle suspended between them on gossamer threads, for all to see. That day, they replaced hope with trust.

I wish them more laughter than tears, more joy than sorrow, and more kisses than curses, because life gives us both. May they always remember how fragile that bottle suspended between them is, and that if they lift a hand to point at the other, it will fall. Instead, may they work as hard as it takes to put the relationship before themselves and enjoy their dream of crossword puzzles and growing old together.

PART TWO: SAY IT

I CAN BE YOUR HERO, BABY.

Y'all had an assignment a few chapters ago. Remember what it was? Hint: a list . . . things your most beloved ones did right . . . no looking for the negative? Raise your hand if you completed your assignment. All you slackers move to the front row where I can keep an eye on you. The rest of you? Good job.

Maybe some of you even took it a step further and applied the concept to yourselves, treating yourselves with more love and kindness, looking for the things you did right. If so, bonus points for you. Now let's build on the great work you did. (Or go back and make your list now, but make it fast, because I'm not waiting on you.)

Looking for the best in others is like pushing a reset button on our opinion of them. It causes us to view them and think of them differently. That's excellent, and it's half the work. The hard half. Now for the easy stuff.

Your next job is to harness the power of your thoughts by reframing how your beloveds think of themselves. How? By telling them and anyone else that will listen about all the wonderfulness that is them, over and over. Email it, put it in a PowerPoint, say it, sing it, post it as your Facebook status, blog it, do it however you want, but just do it.

In life, we create the greatest forward momentum by focusing on the positive. We all know the flip side to this, the danger of creating the negative by speaking it. Parents minimize their children by focusing on their failures instead of their successes. Marriages crumble from lack of respect or too much nagging. Personally, painfully, I can tell you that my awesome relationship with my husband goes through the normal dips, and that those dips are usually tied directly to one or the other of us overcriticizing the other. However minor our complaints may be, they can make our beloveds lose faith that they are heroes in our eyes. And yeah, I do it more often than he does. {Pamela, practice what you preach.}

The greatest strength, though, is in striving for the positive, not just avoiding the negative. So we shan't talk about that negative stuff anymore. Let's turn our bright and shiny eyes toward the goal: praise.

Over the years, my friend Rhonda had sent her husband a number of cards and funny lists of things she loved about him. She found all of them, saved carefully and bound by a rubber band, in his closet. Now why in the world would he save them? Aren't we just supposed to know how someone feels about us once they tell us, remember it, and move on like mature adults with this certainty intact, instead of demanding constant reassurance like needy children?

Yeah, right. Every one of us—EVERY.ONE.OF.US.—has a needy child in there somewhere. Love means (among many other things) taking care of those needs in others. Rhonda's words took care of that for her husband, so much so that he kept them to refer back to any time he needed to.

When Heidi's husband's birthday approached, she wrote her list of everything he did right, and she gave it to him. How do you think he felt? About 10 FEET TALL. Like a hero in Heidi's eyes. Don't believe me? Read her story for yourself.

I've done sweet things for my husband before. Poems, surprise gifts, etc.

But I have never made a list of all the things I appreciate about him. I typed out the first 60 I could think of. He loved his birthday party and his presents.

Afterward, I gave him his List. I started dogging myself, thinking it's not long enough, maybe he wouldn't laugh at #58, etc. But he's awesome, so I really had nothing to worry about.

He stood quietly with one arm around my waist and read through it, chuckling every so often. When he was done, he thanked me and gave me a big hug. That means I did good. I thought he might hand it back, set it on my desk, or maybe file it. No. He pressed it into the shredder.

I'm kidding. Though we both have dark senses of humor and I would have laughed at that, he took it with him . . . and locked it in his safe, where he keeps his collection of silver and gold.

I think I nailed it.

(Number 58: If I really-really wanted to, he'd let me put make-up on him.)

Make someone into your hero. Big 'em up so much that their little hearts burst like Roman candles. Heck, do it for several people. Don't stop until you're completely out of breath. It's like working out—push yourself, and next time it will be easier and you can lift more and run farther.

You'll thank me later. I promise.

THE KEYS TO PAMELOT

***

Poem by me.

***

There's a land of lies and butterflies
Just beyond the sun
The unicorn will take you there
To meet your only one

You'll feast on tears and bitter fears
Manna to your lips
The beauty makes your heart so full

You won't mind when it rips

These are the keys to Pamelot
To Pamelot
To You
These are the keys to Pamelot
My love

A gift that's freely given
Into your eager hand
It's everything your heart desires
Completes you as a man

But when the land is tempest-swept
And crazed with lightning strikes
You may call for that unicorn
But you won't see her twice

These are the keys to Pamelot
To Pamelot
To You
These are the keys to Pamelot
My love

And what, you ask, can free you from the prison of
your love?

Death perhaps, a poison, intervention from above?
But you chose to ride the tempest, and it chose you as
well
Your freedom is to love the storm in beauty and in
hell

These are the keys to Pamelot
To Pamelot
To You
These are the keys to Pamelot
My love

ACCENTUATE THE POSITIVE, ELIMINATE THE NEGATIVE.

I'm issuing another challenge to all of you out there. Are you sick of my challenges yet? Be thankful you're not locked in one of my multi-day classes, where you can't run away!

Listen up, I'm talking to YOU. All of you. Yes, even you, the person who tried to close the book real quick so I wouldn't see you reading me . . . but I did, and I know you can hear me.

The challenge is this: Say something nice to and about your partner (or other loved one) every day for thirty days. Yeah, I know, you made a list before, but that was a one-time event. This is a daily thing. Praise her, encourage him, spotlight her best traits, tell people your favorite things about him. I call it the 30 Positive Days Challenge. Here's how you do it:

1) Make your proclamation 100% positive, no *buts, howevers, or on the other hands*

2) Don't ask for anything in return

3) Make him or her aware of it each day

4) Make at least one other person aware of it each day. It even could be me[9].

Want some encouragement? Let me[10] know you're taking the positivity challenge so that I can send positive thoughts your way. The more of that—positive energy—coming at you, the better, I always say.

You may tell your partner why you are doing it, if he or she asks. You may do it for more than one person, if you'd like. (But Lordy, I hope you don't have more than one partner, or that may defeat the goal of intimacy we are trying to achieve here.) If you don't have a partner, select someone who is important to you, and do it for them.

---

[9] pamela@pamelahutchins.com

[10] Send me an email, or comment to me on Twitter (@pameloth) using the hash tag #30PositiveDays, or on Facebook where I am "Pamela Hutchins, Author."

Why, you ask, would I subject you, dear readers, to this tortuously difficult exercise? Well, I don't think I'm half of a couple who makes you want to puke by accident. I am blessed, and Eric is a fantastic husband. But we know that great relationships take effort, and that the return on investment is amazing.

It's not enough just to see the positive and think the positive. You've got to make your partner hear the positive as well. If I am focusing on Eric's faults (sarcasm, for example, which he is quite good at), then I see sarcasm, and I am unhappy with it. Then my unhappiness shows and translates into less than attractive behaviors of my own; ummm, nagging about the sarcasm, for example. A giant cesspool of negativity forms.

If I focus on how hard he works, and what a great job he does every day without taking his frustrations out on anyone, I see the positive. If I then share the positives I see in him with him and with others, he sees my high opinion of him, he feels awesome, others see my high opinion of him and treat him like a great person, and in general, things go even mo' better for him.

What's more, after this goes on for a while, how do you think he feels about me? Might he, just maybe, look for, think about, or say nice things to me as well? Possibly . . . well, in his case, definitely, because that's the kind of great guy he is.

I'm not making you do anything I wouldn't do myself. Eric and I have done this exercise, too. As we work our way through the next few chapters, I will share ideas with you from my log of Eric's positive traits, how I shared them and with whom, and how it went. And vice versa, his for me.

So, now, Ms. Thing, sitting over there with your girlfriends at Starbuck's, complaining that your husband never sends you cards or flowers anymore, I can hear you. And it's you I'd most like to convince to try this challenge. Yes, really. You. You can do it. I would love nothing more than to overhear you someday telling your girlfriends that your husband is a good kisser, or that you love how kind he is to his mother, or how he always pulls your chair out for you at dinner.

And, you, the one who tweets about what an asshole your husband is? I read your blog, and you griped about him there, too. Man, if it's that bad, maybe you need counseling, or maybe you'd cause less damage apart. I don't know. That's for you to decide. But if it isn't really that bad, why not say so? What are you afraid of? What's the worst thing that could happen if you said something nice to and about someone for thirty days straight?

What do you have to lose?

When Eric and I did this challenge, I wrote this about him on the first day:

> My husband Eric works hard to bring out the best in others, to encourage them, to give them opportunity. I benefit hugely from his efforts, as do our kids. I hope it makes him realize that he is a hero to me, and that I consider him a wonderful and selfless person. I may need more than thirty days, with all I have to say about him!

Now go forth and praise, my friends.

SMART(ALEC)PHONE

My husband traveled to Tulsa for work once while I stayed safely at home, yet business travel woes somehow plagued me anyway. It's my lot in life, since both Eric and I work as consultants. When we travel, most of our communication is by text message, and I rely on my trusty traitorous iPhone to do my talking. Here's how it went while he was on the Tulsa trip:

Day one:
What I typed: "I love you honey"
What iPhone sent: "I love you Joey"
(MY HUSBAND'S NAME IS ERIC)

Day two:
What I typed: "I'm getting into bed"
What iPhone sent: "I'm getting into Ned"

(DID I MENTION MY HUSBAND'S NAME IS ERIC?)

Day three:
What I typed: "I need you here. Please hurry."
What iPhone sent: "I need you here. Please Huey."
(HIS #$%^&* NAME IS EEERRRIIIICCCCCCC)

Apparently iPhone is a promiscuous little beast who thinks I get around like she does; that, or she is trying to sabotage my relationship with Eric. Maybe she's had her eye on him all along.

Lesson learned: Keep your friends close and your enemies closer. And use a Blackberry.

IF YOU DON'T HAVE SOMETHING NICE TO SAY, THEN YOU'RE PROBABLY NOT TALKING ABOUT MY HUSBAND.

Here's my seventh-day update from when Eric and I embarked on our own 30 Positive Days challenge:

Whoa. What a week it has been. Saying nice things about each other in the 30 Positive Days Challenge creates the kind of wonderful feelings that lead to intimacy—physical and emotional intimacy. The "run for the drugstore and buy some Azo" kind of intimacy. Oh, and it's not just me who thought it was going well: on day three, we went to the theater, and a complete stranger asked if we were newly-weds. Cool.

The play by play:

Day 1:

He said: Pamela has been wonderful, caring and loving to my parents.

She said: Eric brings out the best in others, to encourage them, to give them opportunity; he is a wonderful and selfless person.

Day 2:

He said: Pamela is wonderfully relentless on goals. I respect her determination and courage. Great example for her kids.

She said: Eric gets better-looking every year, but is without vanity.

Day 3:

He said: Pamela has an incredible presence, she takes over a room. She has a combination of beauty, intelligence, & careful listening.

She said: Eric has a creative problem-solving mind. We met at work. I thought he was brilliant then, & I still do now.

Day 4:

He said: You can count on her. If she says she will do something, she will. If she says she loves you, she does.

She said: Eric is of Hungarian/gypsy descent: gorgeous dark skin, individualistic, impulsive, good-proud, intense dark eyes.

Day 5:

He said: Pamela has an incredibly beautiful singing voice. It does not come out often, but you can tell when she is feeling good!

She said: Eric is fiercely loyal. Never has anyone taken my side, had my back, & protected me like Eric. I am safe.

Day 6:

He said: She consistently cares about and is good to my kids, even when they are not in return to her.

She said: Eric has a really cute butt!

Day 7:

She says: Eric is an amazingly caring father who invests his time and emotional energy in the development, security, and well-being of his kids, in the face of a lot of adversity, whether or not they appreciate him or show love and caring back to him.

Honestly, how could you not be madly in love with each other after a week of that kind of sharing? It rocked. Our kids think we're dorks and roll their eyes. But they smile.

OK, readers, some of you are participating, but you're afraid to tell anyone, aren't you? Bwack bwack bwack . . . that's my chicken noise for ya. Be loud, be proud . . . of your partner!

SMART(ASS)PHONE

The iPhone and me pictured in happier days.

Latest skirmishes in iPhone v. Pamela:

Eric was in India one November, feeling fat and lazy because he had not been able to run, swim, or bike much in the previous few months. So he texted me about a work success he had, and I typed in reply, "Woo HOOOO!"

iPhone sent him, "Woo HIPPO!"

Then I went to judge a debate tournament. I had never competed in the Cross Examination category, and I hoped I wouldn't have to judge it. After getting my assignment for round one, I texted Eric, "I'm doing PROSE, awesome, that's what I did in high school, so easy."

iPhone sent, "I'm doing ORGIES, awesome, that's what I did in high school, so easy."

After this latest incident with iPhone, I have ordered a Blackberry. Or maybe I should just go back to a land line with rotary dial. Who knew the biggest threat to our relationship would be a smartphone?

(NOT SO)SMARTPHONE

Your choice-see the positive (Eric's message) or see the negative (a mirror I'll have to clean).

Back in the day when we did the 30 Positive Days Challenge, Eric and I had a great second week. That

Saturday night we had dined at a little French restaurant in the middle of Beef Country, USA, AKA Nowheresville, TX. The proprietress and our waiter commented to us as we walked out, "So nice to see a couple holding hands. Quite a contrast to the couple at the table next to you."

The couple next to us hadn't spoken during the entire meal, except to the waiter, and then only grudgingly because they were both so absorbed in their smartphones[11]. And they ate their beef rare, which grossed me out. I imagined I'd smell cow poop any minute, it was so fresh. But I digress.

Maybe that sounds like a perfect Saturday night out to you, but to me, that would stink. I want my partner 100% absorbed in us. I want a conversation. I want to hold hands. I want, yep I do, romance.

Monday we went to the post office to mail our taxes during our lunch date before I flew out to Tampa for work. We were standing in line and an adorable little old lady behind us peered over her half-glasses with the slide-over shaded lenses and said, "You are the cutest couple. It just makes my day to see you." We thanked her and told her how long

---

[11] I could tell them a thing or two about the danger of smartphones to relationships . . .

we'd been together, and she said to me, "Honey, you are so lucky, because he looks at you like a newly-wed." Cue the barf soundtrack.

The power of positive, folks. All I was doing was telling my husband the truth, but I'd focused on the positive, and my focus not only determined what I saw and said, but it shaped how he responded to me. If you'd rather play with your smartphones, don't take on this challenge. Me? I'd rather snuggle nose to nose and play footsie.

Heck, apply it to your kids, too. Don't save all the good stuff for your sweetie—spread it around the family. It works wonders on all relationships. Baby steps are all it takes. You can do it! Go forth loudly, and with positivity.

THERE'S MORE THAN ONE WAY TO SAY IT.

Most of the time, I prefer the traditional forms of communication—talking, writing. But there are obviously more creative ways to communicate. When you're thinking of how to say it with or to your partner, don't leave out the possibility and the power of communicating in nontraditional ways.

Before I go any further, I need you to know I don't believe in zombies, sparkly vampires, the Loch Ness monster, or Big Foot. But I do believe in something. I know there's more out there than my eyes can see or my outer ear can hear. I feel it sometimes. I sense it. Do you? That energy which inhabits an invisible dimension?

Some people never sense it. Others of us have what I think of as an extrareceptive ear. A greater capacity to relate to the energy around us, like the energies from living people, or even from formerly living people. From a million unseen sources that we can't name, but we know exist.

Culture plays a role. In some parts of the world, kids are raised to believe, and so they listen more openly. Eric grew up in the Caribbean, where jumbies — ghosts, spirits — were an accepted and expected part of life. Santería, voodoo, and other tropical-clime practices exist for a reason. People in the islands believe in something they cannot see, and are looking for a way to communicate with it and harness its power. Eric has this receptivity, this special ear, and he really freaks me out when he senses the presence of something that isn't actually living amongst us.

I've got some sort of this sensitivity. I could feel the jumbies at Annaly, our rainforest house on St. Croix. But the more common manifestation for me is that I'm a bit of an empath. You know, like Deanna Troi in the purple jumpsuit on *Star Trek: Next Generation*. That kind of empath. Whether chemically or by my thoughts, when I'm with someone in person, I can get all the way through to them, and I receive much more in terms of energy and connection from them than most other people do.

Yeah, yeah, I know. You think this is crap. But ask people that know me. This little skill makes me quite effective in interpersonal situations, when I am focused. People understand and relate to me, latch onto me, grab hold of the energy I put toward them. It makes me a heck of an investigator, executive coach, and public speaker, but I don't always want to do this. It takes a lot out of me. And when I knowingly open my channel, the drain on my resources from needy folks can almost incapacitate me. I've learned to protect myself in my work and only make my energy, my chi, available when I choose to do so.

The closer I am emotionally to a person, the more powerful this force can be. I can even connect from longer distances with those to whom I am closest. And of course, the more the other person is in touch with the unseen, the greater the energy we can pass between us. I think my husband's similarity to me in this regard was one of the things that drew us together originally, back when we were co-workers and there was no twinkle of forever in our eyes.Once, when we lived in St. Croix, Eric was in a horrific bike wreck and I was ten miles away, cooking dinner up at Annaly. Suddenly I was hit by a blunt force of traumatic energy that literally sent me down on my knees with my hand around my throat. I grabbed my car keys and mobile phone off the counter and without so much as my purse or an idea of where I was heading. I drove at breakneck speed toward town. Fifteen minutes later when I was out of the rainforest and back into cell reception, my phone rang. It was Eric. He had hit a car head-on and was refusing medical treatment. He had woken with no memory of who he was but kept saying he needed Pamela. And I heard him.

After we moved to Houston, we were in a disagreement while I was traveling. I decided to cut my energy off from him and come back to Houston one day early. As soon as I decided, from 150 miles away, that I was done letting him "feel" me, Eric called, scared and angry, asking why I had done it. When I reached the outskirts of Baytown and was thirty minutes from home, I relented. I mustered my energy and pushed it out to him: "I'm here, I love you." Ten minutes later the phone rang. It was my husband asking if I was home, because he felt me again.

`One night while Eric was on a business trip, our 125-pound yellow labrador retriever, Cowboy, woke me up at 3:00 a.m. barking like he was scared and trying to scare something off. This is very unusual. Cowboy sleeps like the dead. He's only woken up to bark two other times in my memory, and both times we thought he had frightened an intruder away. I jumped out of bed and ran to the other side of house, sans cell phone or weapon of any kind, toward the sound of my dog's voice. He was pacing up and down an interior hallway between our side door, back door, and converted garage (which also had entrances to the driveway and backyard). My heart fluttered at the speed of hummingbird wings. What to do? I checked the locks on all the doors. I turned on the lights to the backyard and to the driveway. Cowboy wagged his tail and stopped barking. I stroked his giant head. "Good dog, Cowboy." I returned to bed. The clock read 3:05 a.m. Two hundred miles to the east in a Holiday Inn Express in Louisiana, Eric returned to bed, too. At exactly 3:00 a.m., he had jumped out of bed wide awake to confront what he felt sure was an actual intruding presence in his room. He had yelled "Yah" at the dark, then, a few eerie minutes later he had checked his lock. Before I fell asleep, I texted him about what happened. Before he fell asleep, he texted me about what happened. We received each other's texts at 3:06 a.m.

It doesn't work for everyone, it doesn't even work for us all the time. But communicating through this connection is really cool. It gives those lucky ones of us that can yet another method to say it. So why not use it, if you can?

How's the weather out there?

There are days when I am convinced the universe hums along, powered solely by the projection of my heart's energy. Truly, it does. I can feel it. My heart is that happy.

Then there are days when the world is silent and the sun doesn't show me its face. If it was me that powered the universe before, it is me that fails it now, and brings the fog, overcast skies, and the odd thunderstorm or two.

Ah, the difference between a day when all is right with my husband and one where we've misplaced our mojo. Through both kinds of days, I cradle one thought in my hands: The *Relationship is the most important thing*.

I know how easy it is for me to look for someone else to blame those gloomy days on. If you gave me a minute, I could write you a list of negatives about my husband to rival the list of positives, and he could do the same about me. We are human, and we know each other very well. I could scan the list and say, "Yep, number twelve! Therefore, he is a jerk and this tropical depression is all his fault." I would feel vindicated and justified, for a moment.

But I won't do it.

It's not his fault. I make the choices for me. What to say, how to act, how to react, even how to think. Definitely what to believe. What to expect. What to demand of others and of myself.

I chose him. I chose to commit to him. So today and every day, I choose to honor him. I choose never to bitch about him behind his back (and I haven't, not one time ever, may lightning strike me dead this moment if I'm lying). I choose when to foolishly and destructively ignore the important truths: he loves me, he wants the best for me, he has bad days and slips from his Prince Charming behaviors, but he still loves *me*, despite my occasional impersonations of the Wicked Witch of the West. When I ignore the truths, when I choose to start my thought process by consulting the list of negatives instead of the list of positives, then the dark tornado watch day is no one's fault but my own.

In the middle of the 30 Positive Days Challenge, Eric and I got sideways once. Not quite a hurricane, but more like one of those water spout twister-y things. I had to choke out the positive message on Twitter like a bone from my throat, as did he, and we didn't even talk about them later at home (which is the fun part), so it kinda didn't count.

But I believe wholeheartedly that when you do the behavior, the attitude follows[12]. Did I feel a slight warming in my North Pole heart when I read Eric's positive, public words? Well, yeah, I did. And that sparked a fire that managed to melt the ice chamber. Eric's time and positive words weren't wasted, because they'd created a positive feeling about him in me. Wow, full circle again.

---

[12] I've benefitted from many great therapists, counselors, teachers, mentors, consultants, and bosses over the years, some of whose names I can't even recall. The thanks for this statement and many other concepts Eric and I embrace in our relationship go to Eric Allenbaugh, a fantastic organizational and leadership consultant. You can read more about him at http://ww.allenbaugh.com.

HAPPINESS IS LOVE OF ERIC IN THE REARVIEW MIRROR.

After a peaceful weekend visiting my parents in tiny DeLeon, Texas, the kids and I drove off towards home and Houston, and Eric drove off in the other, to San Antonio for a conference. The next few days apart would give me lots of time to write, but inspiration is a fickle thing. Sometimes when he's gone, missing him floods my pages; other times, I am too flat to write. My triathlon training, especially swimming, usually suffers in his absence as well.

When we were about one mile outside of DeLeon, my daughter Susanne said, "Mom, Eric is behind us with his flashers on, and he's honking."

We could not hear his horn—or his repeated calls to my cell phone—due to the decibel level of her song selection: Jesse McCartney and Dream Street performing "Sugar Rush" (if you haven't heard it, it's as bad as you imagine).

I looked into my rearview mirror, and his emergency flashers filled the frame. For a moment I panicked that he had bad news, but intuition grounded in experience told me otherwise.

"What did he forget?" I asked the kids as I pulled over on the shoulder. My grandmother calls people like Eric "a day late and a dollar short." He's forever forgetting something: keys on the counter, wallet on the bedside table, sunglasses on his bicycle, leather jackets (three and counting) on airplanes.

Opening my car door, I leaned out and peered back over my shoulder. He loped in an exaggerated fashion to our old Suburban, like Rocky at the end of a workout in the streets of Philadelphia. I'm sure the Hereford cows watching from the side of the road were as entertained as I was.

"Mom wants to know what you forgot," Clark announced before either of us could speak.

But Eric already had his arms around me and his face pressed against mine. He spoke so only I could hear, which wasn't hard to do with Jesse and the Suburban as cover. "My favorite Brad Paisley song came on, and it made me want to touch you one more time. I figured I could still catch you."

"What song, the one about the ticks?" I asked. "Eric! There are two kids in the car, and this is a public road, you know."

"No! The one about the yellow pair of running shoes."

"I have two pair; neither is yellow. They're pink Adistars."

"Oh, good grief! You know the one. The one I think he wrote from me about you."

I knew the one. I quit being difficult. "You are so sweet. You drove after me just to tell me that?"

He nose-snuggled me. "And to touch you. And to tell you I love you, and I wish we were heading back to Houston together."

"And you didn't even get pulled over for speeding."

"I was definitely speeding." I could feel his smile against my face.

We held onto each other tight for another few moments, and the kids didn't interrupt us — shocker. My heart thumped its dread of the upcoming days without him, but I knew my fingers would dance happy words across the keys now. Maybe I'd even ride the darn bicycle. I got back in the car and enjoyed the sight of him in my rear view mirror as he walked back to his car. I kept watching as he turned around and drove away.

PART THREE: HONOR IT

My Second-Most Important Anniversary

Now, I could spend a lot of words talking at you guys, the faithful readers still plowing through this book, about why you should honor that which is important to your sweetie, and how. Or I could skip the lecture and tell you through stories. I think it's time for some story-telling.

Let's start with the story of the decision I made a few years ago that changed my life. For the better. Forever.

All those years ago and one day ago, I drank alone for the last time. All those years and one day ago, I drank *too much*, alone, and damaged my relationships and myself for the last time.

The catalyst? My son, Clark Kent the ADHD WonderKid, at the age of eight, told his teacher that he was worried about his mother.

Now, see, I've gone and made myself cry already when I'd barely started writing this story! Sheesh. I hate it when I do that.

Clark's words stopped me cold. I knew what he meant. I knew I drank too many Bloody Marys too often, and that it had started years and years before. I knew my face had puffed up, that I woke up hungover over-frequently, that I cut out of work early to drink wine with my girlfriends, that I acted awful when I was drunk, that I no longer exercised. I knew that a hungover me lacked the bandwidth to deal effectively with my kids' issues, let alone Clark's distressing behaviors and challenges. I knew that and a lot more.

But all that was about me, and I didn't care enough about me to do anything about it. I tried, sure, I tried cutting back any number of times, for all the good it did. But for Clark or my other kids, I would do almost anything.

So I told my boss I would see him in ten days. He didn't ask why, which said a lot. I boarded a plane for St. Lucia and checked into a mind and body spa. I planned a week of rejuvenation while I dried out. I'm not a joiner; I wish I was, but I'm not. AA was not for me. So, St. Lucia, solo.

So what did I really do when I got there?

Got drunk in my room on everything I could find in the mini-bar, all by myself, in a panicked, sobbing frenzy on night one. So drunk that I woke up the next morning and didn't remember falling asleep in the bathtub with the TV on. *Congratulations, Pamela. You go, girl.*

I didn't think I could get lower than I had been after I heard Clark's words from his teacher's mouth, but I did. The morning after the last time I drank alcohol was the lowest point of my life, even beating out my later divorce, the bloody aftermath, and the custody battle that ensued. I despised myself. Not for the first time, I wished I were selfish enough to kill myself. It seemed like that would be so much easier.

For me. But this was not about me. It was about my kids.

So, I picked myself up and put on my too-tight stretchy exercise clothes that used to fit and marched with gritted teeth up 7,000 steps in the heat to the mind and body center. I spent the remaining six days (instead of the planned seven) alone in my mind. My version of Elizabeth Gilbert's year of eating, praying, and loving, I guess. I sweated. I cried. I replayed

Clark's words and my failures over and over in my mind. I felt like absolute crap. I walked the beaches until my feet were as smooth as a baby's bottom. And then I came home dry.

It was hard. So very, very hard.

My husband drank quite a lot at the time, and he didn't slow down for me. The bad marriage I had drowned in booze was impossible to tolerate without anesthetic and contributed to my urge to drink. Most of my friends were heavy drinkers, too, and they viewed my decision to stop drinking as a personal indictment of their choices.

Who was this about, anyway? Right. My kids. I kept going.

I counted the days out painfully, one by one. I again rejected the idea of AA, not only because of my anti-joiner bent, but out of fear of the impact it would have on my high-profile career in our small community. I did it alone, with only one real friend who was aware and still with me *(thanks, Nat!)*, in the middle of the Cruzan-Rum-rich island environment of St. Croix, USVI.

Years later, three months had passed. Alcohol abstinence started getting easier—not a lot easier, but easier. And I felt better, I looked better. I lost weight.

I acted nicer. I became more energetic and productive, crisper. I started running again.

And Clark quit worrying about me. (Tiny little sob again, but I've got it under control now, no worries.)

I am now married to a man who gave up alcohol on our first date. The same date on which he told me I stopped his heart. Eric wasted (pardon the pun) no time in showing me he meant to be my hero, and he is, for more by far than putting up with me writing about his Ironman underwear. *(Woops, sorry, honey.)*

People ask me how I do it all. I don't know. But I do know that a drunken Pamela could not have run five marathons and written two novels in one year while parenting and holding down a day job, even with the world's greatest husband.

And it's not just productivity that the alcohol drained away from me. I have more money for what I need to do as well. I refuse to tally how much I've saved by cutting out booze — it would be too depressing. But I am so grateful that when hard times came to our household and I needed to watch every penny, I wasn't battling myself for the money to spend on wine at World Market.

I know alcohol doesn't affect most people the way it does me. Most people can drink in moderation and still thrive, achieve, and parent. I am happy for them, and envious. My non-drinking is not a judgment of what I think others should do, it is simply what I must do.

I'd love to say that after this many years dry, I never think about drinking, but that is not true. Sometimes I wake up with the sweats, dreaming that I have fallen off the wagon. In those dark moments in the middle of the night, I long to search the house for a bottle of comfort. Every time I travel, the urge strikes, because I used to drink alone in hotel rooms. Now, instead, I sit awake all night, writing to distract myself and praying for the day I never travel alone again.

I don't want to waste another day or night of my life. I want to be the best me I can be 24/7, for my kids, my husband, and finally, for myself. I know only one way to do this, so I will stay true. One day at a time. One year at a time. For the rest of my life. It's the only way.

Gettin' It On

So far, we've Seen It and Said It. Now it's time to Honor It, to honor and respect that which is important to the other. You'll recall with nausea that Eric and I are the proud owners of an ROA, in which we made specific commitments to each other. Remember this part?

Our relationship's purpose is to create a loving, nurturing, safe environment that enables us to

•Make a positive, joyful difference in each other's lives,
•Respect each other's needs and differences,
•Encourage each other's spiritual, emotional, and physical needs and development.

Sounds good, doesn't it? But what does it really mean when it comes to our day-to-day lives?Well, hang on, cowboys and cowgirls, 'cause I'm a'gonna tell ya.

In the second year of our marriage, I took piano lessons, a birthday gift from my parents. I didn't ask for the lessons. My parents gave them to me because my husband was trying to get me to drag my rusty fingers back to the keyboard and, with help from a little steel wool and Rustoleum, play again. For the life of me, I couldn't figure out why.

In his pre-Pamela life, Eric had immersed himself in his passions for triathlon and music (slappin' da bass). When we first got together, I didn't understand that they were an escape for him. I thought my job was to enable him to continue to pursue them. He showed me a video of his band opening for 10,000 Maniacs, and I said, "Cool! Join another band."

Wrong answer, Pamela. He wanted to do it together. Music, that is.

After two years of marriage in which he refused to do his beloved sport, I finally got it about endurance triathlon. I aspired to marathons, and I had done sprint triathlons. Endurance triathlon intimidated me. But unless I participated with him in endurance triathlon, he would never do it again.

What was it our ROA said? Ah, yes: *Encourages spiritual, emotional and physical needs and development.*

Duh, me. I got it. He wanted me to do a Half Iron-man.

So I jumped in with both feet, and we did a Half Ironman five months later. Somewhere along the way, endurance sports became important to me as an individual, too. Although, undoubtedly, I sucked, and still do.

Even after I figured out that I needed to be a tri-athlete for Eric to continue in triathlon, it didn't register that I needed to be a musician for Eric to continue in music. I'm told I'm pretty slow for a smart woman.

I had begged, pleaded, cajoled, and praised his playing. We attended a rockin' reunion with his hilarious high school garage band. We went to see his former bandmates play in their new bands. He was invited to practice and play onstage with many groups. I bought him a new strap with a big smiling sunshine on it, and I talked him through his old playlists. But he just would not open the Fender case and get out his darn bass.

I procrastinated for nine months after receiving the gift certificate for the piano lessons, and I had only three more months before it expired. Eric quit making his gentle inquiries and just let me stew in it. I told myself I didn't have time. I thought of all the things I could do that were less self-indulgent: work, housework, errands, writing, training.

But, again, what did that pesky ROA say? *Here it is: Makes a positive, joyful difference in each other's lives.*

Darn it. Woman up, Pamela.

I booked the first lesson. And Eric glowed.

"I heard a song that we could play together, with Clark on drums, Susanne on flute, you on keyboard, and Liz singing with you," he said before I had even had my first lesson.

He explained his concept of bringing together each of the kids' interests in music into family jam sessions. It dawned on me—finally—that he wanted a family experience. I was not self-indulgent for booking the lessons. Rather, I was selfish in not booking them, because I'd prevented it from happening for everyone else.

After my first lesson, I sheepishly told him that I had to practice scales that night to strengthen my fingers.

"I'll play them with you," he said.

Eric had not brought his bass out in six months. But sure enough, for an hour we played scales together, with him riffing a little every now and then. It was a magical time.

He told the kids about his family jam idea. The excitement level in the house shot up, and they hung out with us while we went through the repetitive and not-very-exciting exercise of putting our fingers to work. The next night at dinner Clark offered to get online and hunt for songs for us to play. Susanne suggested we record a Christmas song on a CD to send with our Christmas cards. Liz sang through the entire dinner, got her choir music, and asked me to accompany her on the piano. The whole atmosphere changed, in a very good way.

We ended up recording a wonderfully awful version of "Deck the Halls." You can still see the craptastic end-product under Videos on my personal Facebook page. Don't believe me? Check it out. I've left it open for public viewing and ridicule.

Every day I get a little smarter about how to be Eric's wife in our blendered family. I enjoy the smile I see on his face now when I say something like "I think we should add Golden Earring's 'Twilight Zone' to our playlist, honey." And even more when we do.

After we get back from bicycling, of course.

THE HEATER

***
Lyrics by me.
***

The wind is blowing hard outside
The sky is churning gray
The thermometer reads 32
It's a very chilly day

The trees are bending, arms extending, leaves are
trembling
Snowflakes teasing, winter seizing, air is freezing

You are here inside with me
My temperature is high
The warmth that I am feeling
Is your hand upon my thigh

The fireplace is toasty
The Jacuzzi does its part
But they're nothing like the feeling
Of your love within my heart

Heads are bending, arms extending, lips are trembling
Hands are teasing, passion seizing, bodies pleasing

The water has grown cooler
And the fire smoldered out
The thermostat has fallen
Yes it's cool inside no doubt

But underneath the blankets
It is summer all year long
Thank you for heating up my life
And giving me this song

CARDINALE

Not everything our beloveds do makes sense. My husband has been a fan of the Arizona Cardinals for over forty years. How, one would rightly ask, could something like this happen to a young boy from the Virgin Islands? Some say he was born the patron saint of lost causes, but it was actually much simpler than that: brainwashing.

Eric spent a lot of time in his earliest years with his Hungarian grandmother, who married an Italian named Cardinale. The family changed their name to Cardinal. They embraced their name and decorated their home with cardinals. Young Eric began his life-long obsession with football surrounded by cardinals, at the knee of a Cardinal. He turned on the TV and saw the Cardinals in their beautiful scarlet uniforms, and could have drawn no other conclusion than the one he did — the Cardinals were HIS team!

He has stood by them in bad times and in more bad times. He has borne ridicule most men could scarce endure. Through it all, he has held his head high, worn the colors, even named his dog after quarterback Jake Plummer. The highlight of 2006 was our trip to Phoenix for the National Petrochemical and Refiners Association annual meeting because . . . we got to go to Eric's first home Cardinals game, in their new stadium no less. (They lost, of course, to the Kansas City Chiefs.) One thing that we're never at a loss for is what to give Eric for birthdays and Christmas. Our bedroom is even painted Cardinal red.

In 2007, we bought a house in Houston in a neighborhood with excellent public schools. You know by now that Eric and I believe there is a hand guiding us in life . . . and it turned out that the mascot for our children's new high school was none other than a cardinal.

Despite his lifelong obsession, Eric had never seen an actual live cardinal bird until we moved to Houston. Growing up in the U.S. Virgin Islands, he'd caught glimpses of them on TV, and he pictured them as red, fierce . . . and large.

One day while unpacking in our new house, I saw a male cardinal through the window. Nonchalantly, I called out to my sweetie, "Hey, Eric, there's a cardinal in our bird feeder."

Eric, whose physique looks like you would expect it to after twenty years of triathlon and cycling, pounded into the living room like a rhino instead of his usual cheetah self, wearing an expectant grin and not much else.

"WHERE IS IT?"

Lost for words, I pointed out our front window and prayed the elderly woman next door was not walking past our house.

"It's awfully small."

(That was Eric that said that, not the elderly neighbor.)

He was crestfallen. The mighty cardinal was a tiny slip of a bird.

But he stayed faithful, and to this day, the Cardinals are a big presence in our lives. As I look out the window into our front yard, I see the most beautiful (obnoxious) cardinal pinwheel in the flower bed, erected originally just to embarrass the kids. It worked great! It embarrassed me, too, and I'm sure, made the neighbors wildly jealous.

However, partway through one football season we discovered the true purpose of the cardinal pinwheel. Eric realized the Cardinals had won every game after we put it in the yard, until we inadvertently broke their winning streak by taking it down for Halloween. They had lost two games before he realized the connection. We got it back up, only to have it blow down in a storm during a critical game a few weeks later, costing them a spot in the playoffs. If we had only known, if we had been able to put it back up before the end of the game, if we had just taken our job as fans a little more seriously and not left our house that day!

BOOGIE SHOES

I am blessed with the love of good friends. Some of them I've never even met, but thanks to the power of the internet and the bond of writers, we hang out virtually. We chill. We share. We bond. We give presents.

My writer friend Heidi upped the ante one year with a present she knew would rock my world: a ballroom dance lesson for Eric and me. We went, we sucked, and we loved it so much we bought more. Or, rather, we pooled my gift bounty and a bunch of nice people made it possible for us to buy more with their generous checks and such.

You would think two Half-Ironman triathletes would find dancing a breeze, but we learned on day one that this dancing shit will wear you O-U-T. I glowed, and Eric sweated like a pig. His face was as red as when I write about his Speedo, seriously. An hour of rumba transformed me from Pamelot to Puffalot.

And our instructors are like freakin' drill sergeants (which I can appreciate, as the family disciplinarian). They won't even let us talk to each other. Or drop our arms — excuse me, our *frame*. Or look at our feet. Or stop if we mess up. Or wear street shoes. It's like we're training for the dorky-white-couple dance-Olympics or something.

Our suede-bottomed fairy shoes.

So, as you can tell — extreme physical exercise + rigid discipline — it's totally our type of thing! We had five lessons left, and after that they wanted us to pay like, oh, a mere trifle for fifteen more lessons. A mere trifle as in fifteen hundred smackers. Yes, you read that right. And with me fresh out of gift money, too.

Five to go . . . could we become proficient in that amount of time? And by that, I don't mean ready for *Dancing with the Stars*, but just good enough that Eric doesn't yell the F word on the dance floor (which we learned is perfectly all right with our instructors, as long as we are safely practicing in their studio) more than once every ten minutes.

So we asked.

OH NO, the studio manager said. No, we could not make you social dancers in such a short time.

We gritted our teeth. Oh yeah, buddy? Just watch us.

So we hatched a plan. Instead of just squeezing in a lesson, we would only go to a lesson if it was adjacent to a free (as in totally without monetary cost) group lesson, and we would attend henceforth all the free parties the studio threw to addictify its unsuspecting clientele, until we ran out of lessons.

Last Friday we took Liz, her boyfriend, Susanne, and her friend Annie to a free sock hop. {And I wore Liz's poodle skirt, y'all!} Only no one else was there when we got there! So they gave us a free group lesson. And then other people showed up, so we had the party after all. We'd been stuck on waltz, rumba, tango, and swing up until then, but that night we burst out after our free salsa lesson into the merengue and cha-cha, too. Hear us roar! We took turns dancing with the kids. Everyone had a grand time. And guess what? Eric didn't say the F word a single time.

Armed with our newfound confidence, I jumped onto iTunes and for only $45, I bought whole albums of ballroom dancing music. We put on our little fairy shoes. We folded our ping-pong table and pushed the weight bench and treadmill back against the wall in our game room. We turned on our music and we DANCED.

So. We're leaving now for our free group lesson and our expensive private lesson. Ready to milk every drop of knowledge out of these high-priced instructors[13]. Because come hell or high water, we are going to be socially acceptable dancers when we finish this program. So there.

---

[13] If you actually met our dance instructor, you would think I was on crack. He is probably the nicest, funniest guy in the world. He can't help it that his boss is the aforementioned drill sergeant (with too much hair gel) and the cost of their program requires a second mortgage. We <3 you, Alex

Happy F***in' Birthday

I love this picture. He hates it. My book. I win.

Many (less than one hundred and more than forty-seven) years ago, my wonderful in-laws Larry and Beth brought their third son into the world on St. Croix in the U.S. Virgin Islands. They raised him in the sand, sun, and surf, with summers in Maine on

Lake Mooselookmeguntic. He learned from them the honor in hard work. He became, like his father, a fearless risk-taker. A man impervious to pain. Loyal to a fault to those who loved him in the fierce way he loved them.

Inside the tough kid whose hair was a little too long, the young man who didn't follow anyone else's rules, the one who didn't wear shoes to school his entire eighth grade year, was the soul of a true romantic. A songwriter. A musician. A guy who believed.

A guy who hates birthdays. His own birthday, anyway.

What? How can a dewy-eyed romantic hate birthdays? That's just wrong. But alas, it is true. Eric hates his birthday. In fact, he wants to kill me so badly for writing this chapter that it's choking him, I promise. If you asked him, he would tell you that the best present I could give him for his birthday would be to pretend it never happened.

I want to make him happy. I want to honor his wishes and desires. I do. But I can't quit celebrating the simple fact of his existence, on this earth and in my life.

Sorry, honey.

Larry and Beth, thank you for Eric. Thank you for the gift of this complex, difficult-at-times, beautiful man. I'm so glad he didn't turn out to be the sweet little girl I'm sure you hoped for after two boys.

Eric, I love you, and you know you'll forgive me, so let's just skip the killing me part, OK? And happy f*&%'in birthday!

RIP, MY FINE-FEATHERED FRIEND.

I am a planner. I plan and schedule and plot, much to the delight of my engineer/cyclist husband, who loves to live by a plan. Even more, he loves for me to make a plan and then for us both to live by it. And what he loves most of all is when the plan I make and live by includes a healthy dose of us bicycling and swimming together. I believe a plan is a structure within which to make reasonable changes, while Eric casts his plans in cement. Obviously I am right, so there usually isn't much of a problem.

But I did not plan what happened to us in the Good Old Summertime Classic, a sixty-nine-mile bicycle ride along some of our most favorite roads for cycling, anywhere. The bike route runs in and around Fayetteville, Texas, including the tiny old town of Roundtop. We had trained for it. We had talked about it with joy and reverence. Eric even accidental-ly went to get our packets a full week before they were available for pick-up (don't ask).

The night before the race, I developed a PMS[14] /hormonal migraine. Because it was the middle of the night, I took one of my gentler migraine prescrip-tions, hoping that this pill plus sleep would be all I needed. I woke up at 5:00 a.m. to the mother of all migraines. I caved in and went for the elephant tranquilizer. Unfortunately, I was so nauseous from the migraine, I couldn't eat. My husband, a man of immense patience and even greater kindness, sug-gested we stay home.

But we had made a plan, so I got in the car any-way under the theory that I had no idea now how I would feel in two and a half hours. Although I kinda did know, and just didn't want to admit it.

I should have listened to my husband.

On the way to the race, driving in the dark, the unthinkable happened. I had my head on Eric's shoulder, sweetly sleeping (make that "snoring and drooling under the influence of the elephant pill"),

---

[14] Technically, I suffer from PMDD – Pre-Menstrual Dysphoric Disorder – but try to say, "I'm feeling PMDDy" or "I'm really PMDDing right now." Yeah. It doesn't exactly roll off the tongue.

when he let out a tiny swear word. Actually, I believe it started with an F, and was preceded by the word "mother," and that his voice blasted through my cranium and echoed madly inside my impaired brain.

"What happened?" I screamed, heart pounding, hand clutching throat, eyes sweeping the road for signs of the apocalypse.

"I hit a cardinal."

OH MY GOD. HE HIT A CARDINAL.

Since the time he could speak, my husband has proclaimed himself a fan of the ~~Chicago~~ ~~Phoenix~~ ~~St.~~ ~~Louis~~ Arizona Cardinals football team. His screen saver at work has always been a giant Cardinal head logo, until very recently when he finally switched it to a picture of us, under teensy-tinsy little applications of subtle pressure from me. He watched their playoff game in 2009 at 2:00 a.m. through a webcam picture of our TV on his laptop in his hotel room in Libya. He collects cardinals and Cardinal paraphernalia and insists on displaying them prominently in our bedroom.

Back to ear-splitting expletives and wife-under-the-influence. "Honey, I didn't feel an impact. Are you sure you didn't miss it?" I asked.

"They're awfully small birds," he said.

Ahhhh, good point. We drove on somberly. We arrived at the race. I stumbled off to the bathroom. When I came back, Eric was crouched in front of the grill of our car. I joined him, confused. He held up a handful of tiny red feathers.

I swear it was the drugs, but I burst out laughing. "You, you of all people, you killed a *cardinal*?"

He glared at me as he picked the biggest and brightest of the small feathers and tucked it reverently into the chest strap of his heart monitor. "I'm going to carry this feather with me in tribute, the whole way."

So we got on our bikes: me, wobbly, cotton-mouthed, and somewhat delirious; Eric, solemn and determined. This, the ride for the cardinal, would be the ride of his life. Sixty-nine miles to the glory of the cardinal.

I made it all of about two miles before I apologized. "I'm anaerobic, and we're only going twelve miles per hour on a flat. I'm really messed up from these drugs."

"You can do it, honey. We came all this way. Now we're riding for a higher purpose."

I gave it my best, I really did, but a few miles later, after a succession of hills where going up with a racing heartbeat was only slightly less awful than cruising down with a seriously messed-up sense of balance, I pulled to a stop.

"I've never quit before, but I can't do it today, love."

A beautiful male cardinal swooped across the road in front of us. Eric bit his lip. "I understand. Do you want to flag a SAG [support and aid] wagon?"

"I can make it back if we just take it easy. I'm sorry, honey."

My husband treated me like a princess that day, but all the excitement had drained out of him. This race we had planned for was not to be. And a teacup-sized bird had sacrificed his life in vain, because I had overdosed on Immitrex and ruined the plan. The waste of it all, the waste of a day, the waste of a life: it was hard to overcome. But Eric tried; I'll give him credit for that, the man really tried.

That night, after we did a make-up ride on the trainer while we watched *We Are Marshall* (interrupted occasionally by Eric's sobs, because the only thing worse than a dead cardinal is a dead football player), I pulled our sheets out of the drier and brought them into our room. Eric—wearing his new Fayetteville Good Old Summertime T-shirt—helped me put the warm, clean cotton on the bed.

As we hoisted the sheets in the air to spread them out over the mattress, a tiny red feather shot straight up toward the light and wafted down slowly, back and forth, back and forth, until, pushed by the soft breeze of our ceiling fan, it landed on the pillow on Eric's side of the bed.

Actual cardinal feather on Eric's pillow.

Steeling myself for the worst, I shot a glance at him to see if he had noticed. I did not exhale. Maybe I had time to brush it off quickly? Too late—he was staring at the feather. "Is that damn bird going to haunt me for the rest of my life now?" But he smiled.

"Probably. You did senselessly murder a cardinal, Eric."

And he laughed. And we began to talk about our plans for the Tour de Pepper ride the next weekend, a ride where, I hoped, we would not cause the death of any of God's creatures. Or at least nothing but an armadillo.

BOOT SCOOTIN'

We christened the Bubba in Eric's Bubba-mon[15] -iker at Billy Bob's Texas in Fort Worth. Now, those of y'all who lack the good fortune of personal familiarity with Billy Bob's, let me 'splain. Billy Bob's holds the title of world's largest honky tonk and has done so for thirty years. It's smack in the center of Rodeo Plaza in Fort Worth's historic stockyards, where you'll see cowgirls on horseback and cowboys lassoing fire hydrants. For reals. We even saw a man leading a rat on the back of a cat on the back of a dog, which was oddly cool, but had nothing to do with the stockyards themselves.

The sheer size of BB's is amazing, but it's what they pack under its roof that makes it a Texas tradi-

---

[15] Eric earned the nickname Bubba-mon as an island-boy transplanted enthusiastically into the heart of Texas.

tion. I mean, hello, at how many bars can you adjourn to watch live professional bull riding? And then two-step a few turns around the wooden dance floor under light reflected off the disco saddle suspended and rotating above you, sweat flying off foreheads under cowboy hats pulled low, boots shuffling, skirts twirling, yee-haws resounding? At 10:30, the other half of the several-acre building comes to life and the main act takes the stage. What's a tuckered-out dancer to do? Grab a beer from the bartender uncapping five Budweisers against her cleavage? Rest her tired feet and enjoy a chicken-fried steak and taters? Or try her luck in the casino area? The place is countrified Disney World.

So, Bubba-mon, armed with five dance lessons and a bride who learned the Cotton-Eyed Joe before she wore her first training bra, hit BB's with a vengeance. The first lesson he learned was that traffic moves fast and in a prescribed direction, like a NASCAR track. If you mess up, you don't stop, unless you fancy death by boot stomp. The next lesson? Don't watch the other dancers. Distractions range from wardrobe malfunctions on women too old to dance in miniskirts anyway, to intimidation from show-off urban cowboys who picked up their skills at some fancypants dance studio (can you imagine?).

I hadn't worn my cowboy boots in years, and I had open wounds within fifteen minutes. Luckily, the gift shop sold Western-themed band-aids, so we kept dancing for two more hours. Eric's casualty was his pride. Now, I have permission to tell you guys that he is a perfectionist who doesn't laugh easily at his own mistakes. Uh-oh. But he kept at it, with me chanting quick-quick-slow-slow at his request through every song. As a bass player, Eric had trouble wrapping his head around the three-count nature of the two-step set to a four-beat measure. (Wouldn't you?) And we didn't learn two-step in dance class; we did fox trot. Similar . . . but, well, worlds apart.

After a half hour of me reassuring him that no one even noticed him in a place this size, a gentleman leaned over to me and said, "Honey, he sure is getting a lot better already." Woops.

But, directionally, he was! By the end of the night, Eric was laughing and singing, spinning me, going sideways, forward, backward, and had even learned to lean back against my encircling arms while I did the same in his, and twirl together. My island boy was country dancing like he was born to do it. (Shhh, don't tell him that 75% of the boys I grew up with refused to ever really learn. I had convinced him that it was a citizenship requirement in Texas.)

I would never try to mislead my husband; perish the thought. Bwah ha ha ha.

Want to capture the feeling at home? Throw some sawdust on the floor, turn on your local country music radio station, and try a little quick-quick-slow-slow around your kitchen. I'll bet you can't last five minutes without a laugh and a smooch.

PART FOUR: DO IT

DOES MORE SEX MAKE IT BETTER?

Short answer: yes. On to the next chapter.

Long answer: yes, and . . .

I read an article on CNN Health's website[16] that touted the benefits of having sex frequently—safe sex, with someone you enjoy having sex with. The author, Elizabeth Cohen, profiled a couple who had sex every day for thirty days. She cited anecdotal stories, scientific statistics, and gave examples of health benefits from having sex every day, too, like that it helped with PMS.

OK, sign me the hell up for this program, I thought. I'm hormonal right now, which means I'm fantasiz-

---

[16] "New Year's Resolution: Have More Sex," by Elizabeth Cohen, January 2, 2010, http://www.cnn.com/2010/HEALTH/01/07/sex.health.benefits/index.html

ing about killing with my bare hands the AT&T U-verse rep who just patronized me on the phone about their crappy service, eating my way through a dozen Cinnabons I bought "for the kids" as a "surprise," and runny-snot sobbing about all of it.

Oops. I digress. Yeah, yeah, health benefits. Lower stress, sleep better, and much more. The couple she wrote about had found it an overwhelmingly positive experience, and the author concurred that more sex seemed to be good for relationships and the individuals in them.

I agree with her conclusion and find it inspiring. Couples should already be doing this anyway. There were a few points the article did not address, however, issues I think are critical to couples.

1. <u>Sex is more than intercourse.</u>

There are many other ways to achieve sexual intimacy than traditional baby-making sexual intercourse, and there are benefits from all these other forms of sexual contact and touching, too. I am a firm believer that humans need touch. And I hope that couples aren't discouraged from physical intimacy if they can't have baby-making sex. Go ahead . . . cuddle, hold hands, rub noses, go a little crazy (safely!), smooch up your sweetie. It will make everything feel better, physically. Get out and Google this if you don't believe me. I'm not going to do your research for you; this one is just too easy.

2. The mental and emotional benefits are as large as the physical benefits.

See #1.

As much as I cringe to think of my husband's life before I came into it, it hurts me to know that until we were together, he was not routinely touched, and that impacted him deeply. He is now the absolute king of touching, the champion of PDA. It's like he's making up for a thirty-year deficit, and I am the lucky recipient.

The result? People tell him he looks a decade younger. He says he feels younger. I can feel it, too. When we touch each other, we can sense the love pulsing between us.

One night as I was hugging Eric, he said, "You're buzzing."

"I haven't touched alcohol in years, so I'm pretty sure I'm not," I said.

"Not that kind of buzzing. Like the buzz of an electrical current. I feel like I'm a battery plugged into a charger," he said.

What a nice thing to be able to do for each other. Think of all the unhappy couples you see, with miles of distance between them, their batteries draining. It's harder to fight with your arms around each other. Give it a try, see what happens.

3. <u>Intimate relationships wither without physical intimacy</u>.

Not just the baby-making variety of intimacy; again, couples that can't couple in an animal-husbandry sense can still touch each other in ways that express love and caring and are fun. But if you can do the deed itself, then do it. A healthy forty-year-old woman once told me that she and her husband only had sex three or four times a year, but that it was always special. The husband's description of their sex life was that if they got drunk enough they would do it out of biological need three to four times a year. Does anyone care to guess whether this couple is still together?

When my girlfriends complain about sex, or boast about how infrequently they have sex, I wonder if they actually believe they are still or will remain the intimate partners of their husbands? Try having sex every day for a month as the CNN article suggests (or substituting intimate touching for intercourse, if you can't have sex). Even if your relationship isn't in great shape when you start, there's very little chance that it will be worse at the end of the month.

The absence of physical intimacy is a serious danger sign. Once, my own father offered his painful view of my (now failed) first marriage to me. At the time, he was coming out of anesthesia post-surgery, so the truth serum was upon him. Mincing no words, he told me that I needed to show my (now ex-) husband more physical affection. He was right. We had a dismal marriage, and my ex somehow was able to discover the love of his life—not me—while he was still married to me. He had so little connection to me that he once left me in the hospital after heart surgery because he was unable to drag himself away from his laptop and come upstairs to sign me out. I don't even blame him. We didn't have a connection, him to me, or me to him.

4. <u>You just have to do it.</u>

Sometimes you don't feel well or something hurts. Eric once broke his back and his pelvis, and was also suffering from injuries to both wrists, both elbows, and one shoulder. And he had a concussion. How he even wanted to have sex, much less was able to, I will never know, but he did. Not all of us are superhuman, of course. But the adrenaline sex brings on actually makes you feel better and sleep more soundly afterward. Read the CNN article for studies on this effect. The exchange of intimacy and caring is a salve to what ails you. If you can, summon your reserves and do it anyway.

Here's to an intimate, loving relationship for you and your partner. The kind that includes sex. Just don't tell me the details, please.

A P H R O D I S I A C

***

Lyrics by me.
***

I stumble out of bed
You hand me coffee on the stairs
I go to do the laundry
But you're already there
I say I look like crap
You stroke my face and touch my hair
You don't even look surprised
When I jump you then and there

You're my aphrodisiac
My aphrodisiac
You show me that you love me and you always got
my back
You're my aphrodisiac

Aphrodisiac

Other men bought fancy dinners
And gave me lingerie
You are much more suave
Than to seduce with chardonnay
You protect me from the wolves
And keep the kids at bay
When I want to write and sing
You make it all ok

You're my aphrodisiac
My aphrodisiac
You show me that you love me and you always got
my back
You're my aphrodisiac
Aphrodisiac

You're my aphrodisiac
My aphrodisiac
You show me that you love me and you always got
my back
You're my aphrodisiac
Aphrodisiac

I think you had this planned all right from the start

You knew how to make me crazy and you took me
all apart
You're gorgeous sexy, baby, but that ain't what
makes me start
I want you, need you, gotta have you, love, you are
my heart

You're my aphrodisiac
My aphrodisiac
You show me that you love me and you always got
my back
You're my aphrodisiac
Aphrodisiac

You're my aphrodisiac
My aphrodisiac
You show me that you love me and you always got
my back
You're my aphrodisiac
Aphrodisiac

SCREW MY BEST INTENTIONS.

The clock read 2:00 a.m. Two hours past yesterday. Four hours before today would start.

Yesterday I had such big plans for my today. Monumental plans, plans to write a piece that would rival the best of my work. People would message me in every possible medium.

Blog comment: "Pamelot, you amaze me."

Tweet: "Keep it up, @pameloth, you're the best."

Facebook: "I want to be like you when I grow up, Mrs. Hutchins." (To the horror of my teenagers, their friends have taken to "following" me and reading about my kids' exploits. It keeps them scared straight.)

Email: "Will you be my new best friend?" or better yet, "Can I be your agent?"

Possibilities had screamed through my mind all that evening, just a few short hours before. I got caught up in the maelström, words tornadoing through my head: *Should I be funny? Thought-provoking? Emotional? Inspiring? Educational? I know – I'll finish the piece about fibromyalgia! No. I'll write about our family betting pool. Scratch that – the topic of today is Becoming (Step-) Momela, The Redux.*

So I sat down at the keyboard. And y'all aren't going to believe what happened next: Nothing. Not one damn thing. *ShiFt.* (I'm not supposed to use actual curse words in my writing, because my grandmothers both read my work, so I'll try to keep it to a dull roar.)

I stared at the keyboard with my death ray glare. I stared so hard the screen sizzled and I could smell the smoke as it rose in tiny curls and disappeared in the downdraft from the ceiling fan.

Appear, oh ye words of wisdom. Chapter, write thyself.

Yeah, that didn't work either.

It's deadline day tomorrow, Pamela. You're supposed to be the psycho who thrives on deadlines, who gobbles up time management for a mid-morning snack.

I slugged cold coffee, which sucked. I had just given up my hazelnut creamy yummy sweetener thingy because my thighs were "swole," as my friend the former NFL linebacker/personal trainer likes to say. Wait, though: that's what he says about muscles after a workout. OK, whatever—my azz is getting big. Again. As it tends to do after I carbo-load for forty-five straight days.

Ah, could I be PMS-ing? I hadn't padded my room yet for the monthly invasion of the body-and-mind snatcher. I needed to warn the kids! I counted the days on the calendar and sighed in relief. Nope. Not PMS.

My writer's block tormented me through the night. What could it be? What rat bastard stole my mo-frickin-jo? Note: *bastard* is a noun of common usage, not a curse word; for the record, *damn* falls in the same category, asshole is necessary to describe exes, and *crap* is a biological function, so none of these words should violate the grandmother rule, unless one of them comes out of the mouth of my kids. Oh yeah, and *hell* is where I'm going if I don't clean up my mouth.

I was getting a headache, and I didn't want to get out of the island of my bed and cross the vast ocean between my bedroom and the kitchen for a glass of water and Excedrin. *Ding.* My iPhone interrupted my death spiral. Thank God. An email from Eric, in India, where he would be for two weeks this time.

"Smile, beautiful. I love you."

A grapefruit-sized lump formed in my throat. I jumped up from my nest of pillows and scrambled across the wood floors, searching in the dark. My hands found the laundry hamper.

You're a nut job, I told myself. *Yes, I know*, I answered. I plunged my hand into the hamper and grabbed air. What a night to catch up on the laundry. What had I been thinking? Eric would be gone for two weeks, and the first thing I did when I got home from the airport was wash every article of clothing, each towel, all the sheets, and every last pillowcase in the house?

I knelt beside the hamper with my hands on the floor, each hand splayed outside a knee. My right hand landed on something soft. Cotton. A T-shirt. I pulled it to my face. *Yes.* The T-shirt Eric had worn early that morning before we left for the airport. It was his black T-shirt with the gold letters, the St. Croix Private School Pirates Offensive Coach T-shirt, the one I always made fun of: "So, does that mean you were offensive, or that you were the coach of the offense? Because it's not quite clear to me . . ."

I made a frantic wardrobe change. The scent memory of my husband hugged me. I wished I'd showered after my earlier and uncharacteristically solo run and bike, because I suddenly knew that I would be wearing this shirt a lot in the next two weeks, no matter how it smelled come morning. Sometimes when I'm sad, though, the shower is the last thing I can force myself to face.

I crawled back into the bed made up with the brown sheets that Eric hates because they leave flannel pill balls all over him. The iPhone dinged again. "All is well here. Safe and sound."

I pulled out my laptop and typed my answer in the dark. Click. Click. Click. Send. It would have to do for now. In the meantime, maybe I'd go out for a Cinnabon and coffee filled with really rich creamy sugary hazelnutty butt-enlarging stuff.

Looking For Love in All the Right Places

When my husband left for India for two weeks, I had sex on the brain. I certainly wasn't having sex on the bed or the sofa or the kitchen counter. I was having no sex at all. So it was that week, of all weeks, that Nan (remember Nan?) and I issued a challenge to each other inspired by that CNN Health article I already told you guys about, a few chapters ago: Nan and I committed to have sex with our spouses every day for a month. Yep, every single day, for thirty days. Then we'd compare the impact it had on our relationships.

Now, I understand this subject is somewhat taboo. Fear not. I won't start sharing anything more intimate than I have so far. I believe in the "closed bedroom door" approach to writing about sex. I know. I'm old-fashioned. You're welcome.

Nan and I have often discussed the elements of great relationships (like both of ours), and more than once this has led to talking about sex, and its importance in a truly Hallmark-card-connected sort of relationship. Neither of us is exactly youthful, mind you. We met in an over-forty writers' group. That just means we've had more years than the flat-bellied tight-assed twenty-somethings to get smart about this whole relationship thing.

Confession: what I want is the so-good-it-should-be-illegal thrill that only a sizzling-hawt relationship can give you. I crave to press noses together with my husband while we talk for hours in the afterglow. I yearn for that "I just can't tear my eyes away from you" feeling. And I've already got that. But it doesn't stay that way by accident. We work at it. It's really fun work, sure, but it is a conscious effort to make time for each other and honor each other's needs, including our sexual needs.

That's where the challenge came in. And now I'm issuing that challenge to you. (Don't look behind you like I'm talking to some stalker in your office, Y-O-U).

The Challenge Deets: For the next thirty days, every single day, make time for and engage in some kind of physical intimacy with your sweetie. You may not jump under the sheets every day, but there's a whole world of fun you can engage in. Hold hands, Eskimo kiss, gaze into each other's eyes, be creative. And you can't keep this plan a secret. You have to ask your partner to participate and commit with you.

Did I mention that Eric and I did this challenge starting when he was in India? So our sexual intimacy required more . . . imagination . . . and technology. I started off by texting him. "I love you. You'll be home in 13 days. Yay!"

I followed up with pictures via email. Note: be extra careful typing in that email address when sending your love over email. I got some great responses back; thank God they were from him.

If you think I'm going to share any of these pictures, you are on crack. OK, just one.

I tried to take a picture of my heart, but I lack an X-ray machine.

I entitled the series "Parts of me that miss you." Ahhhh, isn't that sweet? Anything more here would be TMI, so suffice it to say this went great, and let's move on. [I'm now picturing dirty old men all over the world trying to hack our email accounts. Knock yourself out. They ain't *that* sexy.]

I had prepared for my long-distance seduction carefully before he left. I knew he would work fifteen-hour days in 105-degree heat, so he would not have much left in his tank when he returned to his room at night. I wrote intimate messages for each day of his absence and stashed them in his suitcase, and tucked gifts of varying degrees of suggestiveness and sensuality: a cologne sample tube, a SKOR candy bar, cheap silky boxers. And I bought them at the dollar store, because that's the kind of girl I am.

I showered, lotioned, perfumed, did my hair and makeup and donned his favorite nightie. *Rawr.* I was ready. We initiated a Skype connection. He opened his card. He appreciated my efforts and attire. A lot.

So much so that he fell asleep in front of the computer.

But not until we had connected, truly felt the zing across the golden thread that shot out from Houston across the shortest possible distance to Jamnagar and tied our hearts together.

"Show me your hand," Eric said.

I lifted it in front of the camera.

"Now, put your palm on the screen."

I did.

He lifted his hand in front of his camera and placed his own palm on the screen in India. We couldn't see each other's hands anymore because they were outside of the camera lens, but I swear I could feel his. And my tears? He could see those. And not like that stupid jewelry commercial that runs all the time around Christmas, the one where they put fake tears in the eyes of the actor and actress. The real kind.

Distance—not an excuse. Inability to consummate? Doesn't matter. Connecting on a personal, physical level in a way that shows the other in no uncertain terms how much you want them? Score.

In Which Eric Brings Me Something Back From India

According to Dr. Paul Coleman, author of *The Idiot's Guide*, Intimacy = Sharing + Caring + Connecting

***

Eric came back from India on a Saturday. I bet you want to know how it went.

Did one of you just scream "NO?!?" Don't worry, I'll keep it PG.

The first two hours were fantastic, in a "gosh, I hope nobody gets injured" sort of way. They included gifts: jewelry, beautiful handwritten cards, and a Kama Sutra book as a joke, since we were participating in the challenge. (Holy cow, how would you like to be the models that posed for those photos?)

Soon, though, we had to gather the kids and go to a high school football game. Then, because he'd traveled forty-two hours to get home, Eric fell into a deeeeeeep sleeeeeeep. Me, too—I can't sleep when he's gone.

When we awoke, we discovered he'd brought a stowaway Indian virus friend home with him. He was so sick that I nearly took him to the emergency room. Poor Eric.

But, intimacy = sharing, caring, and connecting. It doesn't have to be ground-moving, even if 3,000 miles separate you for two weeks. I held his delirious hand, I brought cold rags for his forehead, I picked up his prescriptions. I typed his dictated emails. OK, we've got caring and physical connection, but sharing requires *mutual*ity and my husband was near comatose.

So, Eric shared his virus with me, and I got sick, too. Ugh! Not the kind of sharing I'd hoped for. Now we were both sick, and there was no more caring, connecting, or sharing. Unless you call sharing a bad attitude intimacy. Me, not so much. That's how we spent Monday and Tuesday.

On Wednesday, when Eric had recovered just enough to return to work, I had my worst illness day. I called him from the orthodontist, where I had dropped one child off. I needed to go to the high school and pick up another kid and drop him at the orthodontist, then take the first one back to middle school, return for the second and drop him back at high school. Except I was throwing up in the parking lot of the Frost Bank Building at Bellaire and 610. If you were there that Wednesday at 1:30 p.m., you know I'm telling the truth.

I called Eric, and my hero came to the rescue. I somehow made it the three miles home without getting pulled over, even though I looked and drove like a drunk. Eric works only ten minutes from the site of my public puking, so he took over with the kids. Ahhhh haaaaa, sharing and caring do not have to occur simultaneously . . .

That night I was still too sick to sit up. Eric brought our *365 Questions* book to bed. He snuggled up to me. He read the first question: "If you could be reincarnated into another life form, what would you choose to be?" He stroked my sticky hair back from my pallid forehead.

"A dolphin," I mumbled into his chest, which, by the way, smelled like the Obsession cologne sample I had packed in one of his India gifts. It was great to have him home.

"Are you sure about that answer?" he asked.

"Yeahadolphinimsurewhatswrongwithadolphin.
" I really didn't have the emotional or physical strength to give every answer twice, so I might have sounded a wee bit irritated.

"Well, I would choose to be a cardinal, and they mate for life. And you would be a promiscuous dolphin, while I would be a lonely old bachelor cardinal." His tone was pure "Duh, Pamela."

"Fine, I'll be a cardinal, too." Even though I can assure you I would want to be a dolphin. *Men.*

He made noises that I took to indicate that my revised answer, while late in coming, was satisfactory to him. He handed me the book. I read the next question.

"If there is such a thing as an afterlife, what do you hope yours looks like?" I scraped my toes against the sole of his foot, and he curled it obligingly. Eric then gave a long answer, most of which I couldn't hear.

Important sidebar: Eric and his offspring mumble and whisper. I call them the Whispering Hutchins. I don't mean that as a compliment most of the time.

"I can't hear you," I said. Again, might I point out that in my condition, I should have been conserving energy rather than repeating everything?

"I said I'd want to be with you. But I'm not sure I would, with that kind of attitude." He lifted the back of my hair and let it drop, then did it again.

"I hope you're kidding," I sniffed. I wondered if I was going to throw up again. Maybe. Not yet. *Be very still.*

"I'm kidding." His voice sounded playful, and he continued with the hair game, so I decided he was likely telling the truth.

"OK, then."

"Well, what's *your* answer?" he said.

"I would want to be with you, snuggled up like this, but I'd have chosen a cardinal as my form in the afterlife instead of getting the answer wrong."

Eric let out a long-suffering sigh. He took the book and read another question. His hand moved to my upper arm and he lightly pinched a trail along it.

"If you could be a superhero, what powers would you like to possess? That's easy. I'll go first. I'd like to flkjwema;lkdmm."

I said a quick prayer. *Dear Heavenly Father, please help me understand my husband. Just 15% of the time would be enough. That's all I ask for. Amen.*

"What?" I asked.

"Flij;kdf;lkijasjf."

"Seriously, Eric, what are you saying?"

"I'D WANT TO FLYYYYYYY," he yelled in my ear. "What would you want?"

"Bionic hearing." I nipped his chest to let him know I was sort of kidding, but with an edge.

"OK, wiseacre, last question for tonight, and then your cranky butt needs to go to sleep. How would you spend the perfect summer day?" he asked.

"It's really hot in the summer and there are lots of bugs. I don't want my perfect day to be in the summer. I like the fall." I nestled further into the crook of his arm for a better sleeping position, which was futile, because someone had to get up to turn off the lights. *Rats.*

"Why don't you just let me answer this one, and you concentrate on being very, very quiet and sleepy?"

This man is smart. "OK," I said.

"I'd spend it in a cabin with you, somewhere cool and beautiful with no mosquitoes, and a giant bed and a fireplace. We'd get up and ride our bikes —" he held up his hand to quiet me as I started to interrupt, "after sleeping in and doing all the things we haven't been able to do for the last three weeks, and we'd ride our bikes on smooth roads with no cars. We'd see lots of animals. We'd hike to a gorgeous stream, have a picnic, and nap on a blanket. Someone would bring us dinner that we would eat outside by a campfire while we snuggled in a double lounge chair and looked at the stars."

I smiled. I know he felt my lips curl up against his chest, because he put his mouth in my hair and said, "So, could you hear me OK down there? Would my summer day be OK with you?"

"It'd be perfect with me."

"Hey, you know when you get better, we'll only have eighteen or nineteen days left on this thirty-day challenge? I'm thinking we're going to have to use an average number for our final total. What do you think?"

I pretended I was asleep and snuggled closer. I didn't fool him. He was probably right.

TAN LINES

I have been threatening a scandalous exposé about my husband, and the time has come. The following is an actual conversation between us.

"Honey, you look like one of those double-stuffed Oreos from the back, except you're milk chocolate instead of dark chocolate," I said.

Eric shot me a look over his shoulder. Not an appreciative-of-his-wife's-sense-of-humor kind of look.

"Whaaatttt?" he asked.

"You know, baby, your tan lines. From swimming."

In the summer, Eric swims at noon two to three days a week, outside. He wears knee-length jammers, and the good Lord blessed him with fast-tanning olive skin. I love holding hands with him when his fingers are like the latte and mine are the steamed-milk topping.

"Very funny. Don't write about that." He hopped into the shower.

"Oh, I wouldn't write about that. If I did, people would be thinking about your naked hiney."

"Exactly."

"Yep."

"So, to be clear, you are promising me you won't write about my tan lines?"

"That's what I'm saying. I think people would be *offended* if I wrote about it. Children might see it."

"OK. Good. Thanks."

"Yup. You're welcome. But I'm not doing it for you. I'm doing it for my readership."

"Whatever, just as long as I don't see some picture of my naked ass that you took as I ran from the shower some day."

"As if. I have scruples, you know."

My appreciation for said unclothed posterior is well known in our family. One day I accidentally texted about my appreciation to his then-twenty-one-year-old daughter, who forever more has called him Sweet Cheeks and Honey Buns. She gets a kick out of it. Him, not so much.

I keep telling him it could be much worse. At least I really, really like him.

"What if I didn't like you, and I wrote about *that*?" I asked him once.

"What if you didn't write about me at all?"

"Then you wouldn't know whether I liked you or not!"

"It's a risk I would be willing to take."

I don't think he really means it. So, anyway, I just thought y'all would enjoy the photo below.

Photo taken of LCD advertisement at Hobby Airport in Houston

No, this is not actuall Eric's butt. His is *at least* ten times better; he may be a year or two past twenty-seven, but he is a workout fiend, which is not without its benefits. This is exactly what his tan lines look like, though. And he does have this bathing suit.

Meow.

Kidding. Of course he does not have *this* bathing suit . . . but pictures do exist of him in a Speedo, and the ever-present threat of me publishing them through the interwebs hangs like a guillotine over him. There's a reason he's so nice to me: fear.

THERE'S AN OLD FLAME BURNING IN MY EYES.

I'm happiest when my husband looks at me this way.

You know how sometimes when you look at the sleeping face of your beloved, you feel like your heart could just burst? That's how I felt while we spent thirty days reminding each other, in a very physical way, of that feeling. We had a blast.

Instead of wowing you with words, I thought I'd show you what it looks like. You know what I'm talking about—that flame that leaps out of your partner's eyes and just burns "I love you MADLY" into your heart. Do you still look at each other that way? Maybe it would be fun to light that old flame up in your eyes, and see how it would make your lover feel, to have you look at him or her that way again.

I *see* the flame in his eyes in the picture in this chapter. And I see it when we look at each other, still. One way we up the intimacy from time to time is to look at these wedding pictures together, again, and relive our favorite memories. It makes the fire burn scorching hot.

Go ahead. You know you want to. Pull out your best of the best, and let the old flame burn.

JUNK IN THE TRUNK

One night, sexy Rico[17] Suave donned his red mating-call very-briefs and dashed to the bathroom,
giving his beloved a few moments to still her beating
heart. He came back out around the corner, stopped
for a moment to flash the light on and off while he
struck a few freeze-frame poses designed to put her
in the mood, and then leaped into bed. It was not a
night for subtlety!

Rico wrapped his woman in his arms, and she
responded gratifyingly by putting her right hand on
his gorgeous left bun. Rico became even more enthusiastic, but soon noticed a change come over his lady.
"Mi bonita, cual es tu problema?[18]" he queried.

---

[17] Rico is Eric in Spanish. It's not his favorite nickname,
but sometimes, well, it *fits*.

[18] "My pretty one, what's the problem?"

Silence, a giggle. He felt a strange sensation as something seemed to be drawn upward out of the back of his mating-call trunks. He turned on the light. With a grin, his wife pulled the rest of the toilet paper gently out of the back of his drawers and handed it to him. He tossed it aside, tossed her over his shoulder, and continued his conquest.

KISS AND MAKE UP OR DIE TRYING.

Thirty days. Thirty frickin days of real life: dogs with fleas, kids with issues, travel, illness, wrecked cars, work, errands, traffic, and a humdinger of a disagreement. How do you sustain physical intimacy for thirty days through all of that, the everyday crap that drains the romance from our souls and the libidos from our bodies?

You don't.

I hear you: "What the hell did she just say? Isn't this the woman that challenged us all to attempt this thirty-day stuff, and now she says *this*?"

I know. But you can't. Not every minute of every day. I'm not in it for the short run, though. Are you? The short run is composed of seconds, minutes, hours, at most a few days. Tiny pieces of our life — important pieces — but not the sum of It.

So here it is, folks, one simple rule for keeping the train on the tracks, the intimacy in your relationship over the long run: Do the behavior of physical intimacy and the attitude for intimacy will follow.

That's all. Do the behavior of love, of patience, of forgiveness, of affection . . . and the attitude of love, patience, forgiveness, and affection will follow sometime soon. As will the higher probability that your beloved will do the behavior right back at you. If you cradle your hurt in your hands, staring at it, talking to it, caressing it, cherishing it . . . you're going to lose a lot more than minutes or hours.

If you put that bad boy down and *do the behavior*, in no time at all (compared to the lifetime you are sharing together), you will kiss and make up. Which in itself can be a behavior to do with an attitude that follows.

And what's not to love about that?

THE END IS THE BEGINNING.

And so, once upon a time, Nan and I entered a faux war to find out which of us had the most amazing, intimate relationship with her fabulous husband. Secretly, we each knew it was no contest. As I sit here writing about it now, I have big goober-y tear tracks on my cheeks. Not sad tears. Emotional tears. Happy, grateful tears.

Sometimes Eric and I marvel at our blessings. Other times we wish our path was a bit less steep and rocky. While these sound like polar opposites, they are not. That's how it is for most of us, isn't it?

When I did this challenge, I didn't know how hard it would be. I didn't know my husband would spend twenty of the thirty days on the road, half of it in a time zone ten and a half hours ahead of mine. I didn't foresee that we would each get a stomach virus and *then* the flu.

The challenge came on the heels of my athletic husband enduring nearly two months with no exercise, on a liquid diet, undergoing medical procedures and vicious migraines for weeks on end while his body refused to metabolize medicines and he had to abstain from even over-the-counter pain relievers. Worst of all, his old bike-wreck-related, knock-you-to-your-knees back pain returned, prompting yet another procedure. He missed day after day of work and fun and training as he sat in clinics and hospitals. He was unable to release his stress through exercise, his normal way of producing endorphins.

I couldn't have known Eric's oldest son would total his car and call us for help. "Umm, Dad, can you come, like, now, please?" I couldn't know that Eric's father would spend the entire month in the hospital with fragile health, and his mother would bear a heavy load, emotionally and physically.

I lost my ability to run nine months before this Challenge. Up till then, I'd been running sixty miles every week. At the time of the challenge? Zero. I had only just beginning to see a future for myself as a runner again. Plantar fasciitis sucks.

I had thrown myself into a void where I announced, "World, I am a Writer!" because I am, but the self-esteem issues I experienced, the up and down, sob, laugh, sob, laugh, is punishing. The hours I spent trying to earn a sufficient income while devoting myself full-time to writing — because it takes that kind of devotion or you will not make it — tired me out.

And then there were the "all the time" issues. Dealing with my ADHD teenager? Exhausting. Dealing with myself, a peri-menopausal woman driven crazy by hormones 33% of the time? Worse.

I don't talk about these things most of the time. I usually go for the laugh, I look for the funny, the positive. I work hard, I love harder, and whining — even about stuff I maybe could whine about a little — is not something I allow myself to do, because it messes up my focus and changes what I see.

But now I share the negative briefly before I put it back in its little box, because I want you to know something that requires contrast to adequately convey. My life is perfect. It is P-E-R-F-E-C-T. I would not change a thing. I have everything I ever dreamed of, because God completed me with Eric, with a partner, a lover, a champion, a husband, a best friend.

I want to share a question we answered from the *365 Questions for Couples* book: "If you could live this life over again, what type of person would you try to be, and where would you reside? Would you make the same decisions this time?"

I thought about my answer for a long time. I relived all my painful mistakes. I cringed at my ignorance, my lack of humility, and my insensitivity. Oh my gosh, could I really have a do-over? I'd rock it this time!

But then I realized that if I changed one thing, one tiny detail, that I might not have ended up sitting with Eric at this moment, reading this stupid question and agonizing over my answer.

So, my answer: I would change nothing. My life has been and is perfect, because it led me to where I am today.

The real questions are these: For the rest of my life, what type of person will I try to be? How will I live my life? What decisions will I make?

And the answers to those rocket out of me, no thinking required. I want to live a life of gratitude, I want to cherish my blessings, I want to focus on the positive, I want to find a way to laugh, I want to be a great mother, and I will do anything — ANYTHING —

that will keep the intimacy between this man and me alive.

I will fall short. I will be a PMS-y bitch. I will lose my temper and scream like a banshee. I will get a rejection letter on a book and sink into days of funk. I will pull to the side of the road in the middle of a bike ride on a perfect day and sob because my whole body aches from the poison of these damn hormones, ruining Eric's day in the process of trashing mine. I will lose my patience when Eric falls short of perfection.

But I will try. I will try so hard. I will never quit trying. And I will always show my husband I want him. I respect him. I believe in him. I am grateful for him. I love him.

The challenge was the best month of my life, up until that point, and the next topped it, as did the month after that. Because it's not just about thirty days. It's about a lifetime of days, till death do us part.

PART FIVE: BE IT

Two True

This is a chapter for those of you who are in relationships with other humans: friendship, familial, domestic, marital, occupational. You know, one human interacting with another human. It is also for those of you who are *not* in a relationship of any kind with another human. Maybe especially for you.

Every day and every interaction presents a fresh chance to see the world differently. Luckily for Eric and me, most of the time we are simpatico. Sometimes, though, one of us gets our sensitive little feelings hurt, and then the most *shocking* turn of events occurs: we immediately process and recall the exact same situation in a slightly different manner.

In my work, I see a lot of dysfunctional relationships. In my private life, I see people who care deeply for one another damaging their relationships, sometimes past the point of repair. And in my marriage, I experience two highly sensitive, self-centered adults loving each other madly, yet occasionally acting like they're playing Whack-a-Mole.

In Whack-a-Mole, the gamer uses an actual mallet to beat the heads of pop-up moles, sending them scurrying back into underground hiding. The game is a mainstay at Chuck E. Cheese's, a place I imagine to be a lot like Hell: full of screaming children, soggy pizza, overwrought parents, and flashing lights. I try hard to keep our relationship from resembling Whack-a-Mole too much, but sometimes there's more overlap than I'd like to admit.

Consider the following real-life example.

I said, while riding a bicycle in front of Eric, "I feel fat."

Eric answered, "Honey, think of how far you've come and be proud of yourself. You look great. You don't even have those fat little places behind your knees anymore. I can see your handlebars on either side of your butt."

Every one of you heard the screech of the needle across the record.

At that moment, I had a choice. I could look at what he said from his perspective, giving him the benefit of the doubt and remembering he loves me and is a nice person, or I could take his poorly considered and horrifically worded statement and club him over the head with it.

Outcome A:

"What do you mean by that? Because it sounds like you are saying I was really fat and I'm less fat now, and that hurts my feelings."

"No, I meant look at how far you have come in our triathlon training. You're not fat. You're beautiful, and you're strong. And you know how when anyone gets out of shape that place behind their knees gets flabby? Well, yours isn't. It's tight. Your hips are tight, too. How can you possibly think you're fat when you're in such good shape?"

(Sniffling.) "I don't know. Maybe I'm hormonal. It's just that when I lean over on a bike I can feel my stomach roll over. I can't help feeling this way."

"Well, it's all in your head. You look great to me, all the time, not just now."

We have had a million conversations that went just like that. I know that is truly how he feels. However, on that day, it did not go well. That day, I took another path.

Outcome B, the real conversation:

"What fat little places behind my knees? How long have you been forced to endure the hell of having a wife who had fat little places behind her knees? And an ass that was so big it blocked out the sun?" {WHACK}

"That wasn't what I meant."

"You know what? I don't want to talk to you. Leave me alone." {WHACK}

"I'm sorry, honey, I think you're beautiful, and you're not fat."

"I said leave me alone." {WHACK}

(After a long pause): "Whatever. You're completely irrational." {WHACK}

I didn't speak to him until we pulled up to the car, and then I spewed out my stored-up hours of angry, self-justifying thought-poison all over him. He informed me that I had lost my mind and he had done nothing wrong, and, by the way, that wasn't even what he'd said. We had an epic verbal throwdown on the side of Farm to Market Road 1488 outside Waller, Texas. We whacked those poor little moles so far down into their holes they came out on the other side in China.

Years later, even hours later, the mediator in me could step back and see the interchange for what it was. What was it I said early on in this book about "HR consultant, heal thyself?" *Sigh.*

Had Eric said something dumb? Undoubtedly. Was Eric an asshole who thought I was fat, wanted to hurt me, and who was lying about me misquoting him? No. Was I completely out of left field to have my feelings hurt, and was I a liar for restating his words in a way he did not agree was factually accurate? No. We were two humans who saw the same event from his and her own perspectives, and the further away in time and emotion we got from it without closure, the more we polarized to our corners, justifying our feelings with distorted memories and discarding the one great truth in favor of our own version.

What is the one great truth? That we are both good people who care about each other and have a long history of positivity and caring.

Had I but filtered Eric's ham-handed statement through the assumption that whatever he meant, he meant from a place of love, and consistent with what I knew to be his true feelings and beliefs, I could never have concluded that he intended to cause me pain, or that he thought I was a hippopotamus on two dangerously laden, totally squished wheels. Had he filtered my reaction through the assumption that I was sincerely hurt, that I honestly misunderstood what he meant, he could never have concluded that I was a nutjob who was deliberately twisting his words.

And we would not have wasted precious energy and hours angry with each other, ripping at the fabric of our relationship, adding a bad memory to our wonderful story, driving our inner moles underground and into hiding from each other and our relationship. We laugh now about the fat little knees and ass that blocks out the sun moment. But it took us a long time to get over the hangover from our fight, like a bad tequila binge. The little moles were scared to come out.

Little moles on bad tequila, an ugly combination. And not a great intimacy or relationship builder.

Think for a moment about someone who is in (or used to be in) your life, someone with whom you have had issues. Have you ever found yourself getting further apart instead of closer as you tried to resolve the issues? Have you ever reached the point where, despite having mountains of good evidence about the person and your relationship, you decided that he or she was a liar? A bad person? A jerk?

Could you have substituted a greater truth instead? Maybe the other person was no greater a liar, bad person, or jerk than you were, maybe instead s/he was simply a human whose memories and feelings were naturally polarizing to support a *position*, just like yours.

So what is true? You have one truth, your compatriot has another. You both have invested mightily in your truth being the one truth; you believe your truth. By now, though — suck it up and hear me well, people — neither of those two "truths" is true. There was a truth, there is a truth, but it is often not what either combatant espouses. And there is a greater truth — the body of truth at the core of the relationship, that deep well of memories you can draw from, the fresh water you can dump on the smoldering heap of dog poo that you've pushed back and forth at each other.

Dump the justifications. Find the truth. Mend. Heal. See the best in each other. Whatever you believe you will see, well, there it will be. Choose to see the best, and you will find it is the truth. Only then can you Be It.

THE RUSH OF TIME PAST MY FACE

***

Poem by me.

***

Wind whips my hair through the window
There you are in the road ahead
Now framed in the rearview mirror

I pump the brakes
I always wanted a fast car
Now I'd rather walk

Maybe if I just roll the window up . . .

BIG LOVE AND THE
CRACK BABY

My husband asked me to marry him one morning, and I said maybe. Usually when he asks — and he asks often, he's romantic that way — I say yes. But not that time. That time I was still in the jet wash of a big love blow-up.

Big love. That's what we have, a big love with big emotions and big hearts at stake. We're pretty poorly equipped for it: two middle-aged losers at marriage their first go round, with the kind of baggage that inspired Miranda Lambert's song "Baggage Claim."

Some people have love, but not big love. Some people don't need or want big love. It seems to me that for a lot of people, life is perfect without the highest of highs, because they appreciate the consistency of a love without the lowest of lows.

Not me. I want the Fourth of July and Christmas rolled into one, even if the price is the occasional shredded gladiator on the floor of the Colosseum. And I have that; boy, do I have that.

How does one survive a big love? Our ROA helps, as does the groundwork we put in to create it. Padded walls help. Valium. Valium is good, too.

What helps most, though, are perspective and a good sense of humor, so that when the big lumps come, we can be big boys and girls and get over it. Get back to the Being of It.

Eric and I go weeks, sometimes months, without a ripple on Lake Placid. (Well, it has ripples, but those are more the waterbed kind. Good ripples.) And then something comes along, and BAM, tsunami. It's that sudden and that random. In my past life, I had a predictable relationship—predictable 24/7 bickering that my children still refer to and roll their eyes about. This is different. Different in an enormously wonderful and scary way.

So why did I say maybe when he asked me to marry him, that time? Eric did something that hurt my feelings. No biggie. He didn't mean to. Three days later, he was contrite, and I realized both his good intentions and my contributions to the misunderstanding.

But this is big love, and it became a big deal. Except that what we battled over was not whether or not he did something wrong, or whether or not I was too sensitive. We fought over the crack baby.

He took it by his action, I took it back by my reaction. The crack baby is like a feel-good teddy bear, only more addictive. It's not like a literal crack baby, which is a serious thing when it happens, and is real, y'all; I get that. *This* crack baby is like a make-believe Raggedy Ann stuffed with crack. The crack baby is an element of our relationship. It's the high we get from loving each other.

Our whole damn fight was literally over nothing more than "make this bad feeling stop and give me my good feeling back." Which would have happened in an instant, if either of us had simply done that. Stopped.

It ain't easy being this difficult. You could strive and strive and probably never achieve these lows. It's a special madness reserved for the truly noble: yours truly, and my beloved.

We get apocalyptic, blasting things along the lines of "My best will never be good enough for you," or "You ALWAYS—" and "So I'm never kind/caring/insert-your-word-here, that's what you're saying?" Nonsense shit. Grownups behaving like children. *Waaaah, give it back or I'll throw a tantrum!*

Sometimes one of us will pull out the ROA, and we'll regroup and handle things appropriately. Other times, one of us will try that only to get thwacked over the head with it. But we usually forget all about the rules in the heat of the moment.

When we are worn out, beat down, and busted, it will finally occur to one of us that we're simply in withdrawal. The crack addict in me uncurls from her fetal position and stands up to survey the damage. It's ugly, but the sun is shining, and look! There it is — the crack baby on the floor. I scoop it up and hug it, and it is gooooood. I let Eric have a turn holding the crack baby, too. All better. Then we can laugh about it and share the guilt and shame over having gouged each other's eyes out (again) for nothing. Except it's not for nothing. It's for fear of losing each other.

As soon as we sober up and can see each other clearly again, we work fast to avoid that self-fulfilling prophecy: while the wounds are still fresh, we talk about how we deviated from our ROA. We hold each other. We apologize. We forgive.

If we are having trouble stopping the tussle, we allow one holler of calf-rope,[19] a privilege that comes with a price. As with ending any of our infamous disagreements, we have to recommit to solving the issue (if there even *is* a real issue, instead of just a crack baby issue), reaffirm our love of each other and commitment to our ROA principles, and release the crap that is dragging us down.

We have to let it go and get the hell over it, which isn't always easy, because we've created a mountain of garbage out of nothing. But we always manage to do it, because we have big love. We have perspective. And eventually, we can laugh about it—with each other and about each other. I tend to get there sooner than Eric, but he gets there a few days later, loud and real. Then we can return to the Being of It.

Big love = epic adventures, big screen romances, and greeting card sonnets. It's Disney. It's *The Notebook*. It's Jack and Rose on the bow of the Titanic. Not everybody wants it, and it doesn't come free, but I wouldn't trade our passion for predictability. I'm crazy that way, and imperfect to boot, and damn

---

[19] Stop hostilities immediately, by saying calf-rope. From the Dictionary of American Regional English: http://dare.wisc.edu/?q=node/71

lucky to have someone who's crazy and imperfect in just that same way.

I'm thankful for the big love. And Eric—the answer is always yes.

OLD FARTS' DATE NIGHT

Date night is a revered tradition at our house. No ruts for us -- we're always looking for a new activity. One month, Eric planned a surprise for me. When I got to the car, he handed me a package. Not a gift-wrapped package, mind you, because he's still a guy, but a bag of "stuff."

"What's this?" I asked.

"Clues," he said, his eyes dancing.

I reached into the bag and pulled out a Journey tank top, complete with a few rhinestones, and a "mix CD." *Mom, Journey is a rock and roll band.*

"Put the shirt on," he instructed.

It barely contained my enthusiasm, if you know what I mean. "I'm a little boobylicious for it," I said, ripping off and bastardizing Destiny's Child all at once. "What size did you get?"

"Um, medium, I think," he said, the quiver in his voice betraying his terror at the subject. The previous Valentine's Day he had *accidentally* purchased me the Size XL package of the Pajama Gram. I wear an 8. After I quit sobbing, I had to admit that I looked pretty funny in the giant tap pants. Ever since then, Eric has erred on the side of too tight.

"Well, that should have fit," I conceded. It would just do for public wear, but I'd keep an eye out for *Fashion Don't* photographers. "Thanks, honey." I kissed his chiseled cheek and caught a whiff of Calvin Klein Obsession. I loved date night.

"I think it looks good," Eric voted. See above: he's still a guy.

We got in the car and popped the mix CD into the changer. Steve Perry immediately sang to us about "Lovin', Touchin', and Squeezin'."

"Those are your hints," Eric said, and he put the car in reverse.

"I think my husband is awesome and he's taking me to see Journey!" I squealed. I had loved Journey since high school. Everyone in the 80's had some Journey song or other as "their song" with their high school boyfriend or girlfriend ("Open Arms" or "Faithfully" ring any bells out there?), and then had

"Separate Ways" as the inevitable break-up song three weeks later.

Eric smiled and turned up the volume.

Two hours of Houston rush hour traffic and three near-collisions later, we made up it from our home southwest of downtown to the Woodlands amphitheatre north of the city. By then, I was a little nauseous, hoarse from trying to hit the high notes with Steve Perry, and no longer sitting up extra straight to fight the inevitable blue jeans shorts and tight tank "muffin top" look. Eric had brought ice cold *Monster Absolutely Zeroes* with us as road pops, and the car had taken on the distinct odor of Monster burps. His, not mine. Because I'm a lady. And you thought beer drinkers were bad, huh?

We parked and started our long walk in. The concert was in the summertime, which in Houston means steam bath, so within minutes sweat trickled then flowed down our legs. But it was OK, in fact, it was nirvana. We were together, and we were going to see Journey, which Eric had picked out just for me. We swung our joined, slippery hands as we chatted. The nausea had worn off by this point, and I started noticing the other concert-goers. And they weren't wearing Journey t-shirts.

"Eric?" I said.

"Hmmm?" he answered, and slugged some more Monster.

He let out a tiny belch, and I leaned as far away as I could get. "Did you notice the car with the Union Jack flag on it parked by us?" I asked, fanning my hand in front of my face as I spoke.

"Nope." He didn't seem curious about it either, or cognizant of my reaction to his odor release.

"How about that one?" I pointed. "Or that t-shirt?" I pointed again.

By now, I had figured out something that Eric hadn't yet realized. And it was something even better than going to a Journey concert. It was "thinking we were going to a Journey concert when we really weren't" and all that implied about the years of fun I was about to have on this issue with my husband.

Eric stopped, and two people bumped into us from behind.

"Sorry, sorry," I said to them, and pulled Eric one step off the path to stand in the dirt while he cogitated.

"Oh, shit," he said.

"Oh, shit," I agreed.

"It's pretty ironic when you go to an old folk's rock concert...." I said.

"Classic rock," Eric interrupted.

"Potato, potahtoe," I said. "Anyway, it's pretty ironic when you go to an old folk's rock concert, and you can't even remember the name of the band that's playing."

My husband doesn't always laugh easily at himself, but this time he did. "Alzheimer's. Dementia. General old age. Or something."

I leaned in for a clench, and we mingled sweat as we hugged and rocked. I leaned into his ear and sang, "Pour some sugar on me," and was given a love-punch for my efforts.

And we continued our walk into the Def Leppard concert in my tight Journey t-shirt, for another perfect date night.

Peace Out

Peace doesn't always flow like a river at our house. Between kid drama, puppy drama, work, finances, and health issues, peacelessness sometimes dams up the waterway and creates a dark lake of ugh, especially for my husband. He had also learned he had an infected abscessed tooth and needed to go on antibiotics and have a re-root canal. When Eric discovered the abscess, my friends were concerned. They warned me that infections of the teeth can impact the heart, the brain, and other organs. It turned out they were right.

After the first round of antibiotics, Eric's fever and health were worse, not better. His endodontist started him on a stronger antibiotic and punted him to an oral surgeon, who couldn't get him in for two weeks. In the meantime, the endodontist didn't tell Eric not to run — possibly because he didn't know that running had been elevating Eric's pulse recently. (I suspect there was also some crafting of the report Eric gave me about his restrictions.)

We went for a run together a few nights after starting the new meds, and from the get-go, my super-fit husband had tremendous difficulty. After two miles, he was drunkenish, weaving, staggering a bit, glazy-eyed. Our pace was middlin'-turtle already, and I knew I had to make him walk. But only a fool would tell Eric to stop mid-effort.

I know well that Eric hates to stop. He feels exercise is critical to his physical and mental health, and his stress had mounted to peak levels in the past two months. His youngest daughter had left for college, his stomach procedure and then this mystery illness had made it difficult to work out, and he was still undergoing pain treatments and epidurals for his back, which was broken in a bike wreck in 2006. He was never able to fit everything he wanted to do into a day, and frankly, he felt like crap and hadn't dared to admit it. The weight of it all was crushing his usually ebullient spirit.

So, how could I get him to stop running without making a bad situation explosive? I slowed to a walk and made a dramatic show of scratching mosquito bites. Eric slowed with me.

"Are you ready to restart?" he asked, in a spot-on imitation of Johnny Depp à la *Pirates of the Caribbean*.

"Welllllllll . . . my feet really hurt. I've been slacking off for five weeks, and this distance is too much for them. Gotta be smart, build them back up. I'll have to walk." When in doubt, blame it on the Plantar fasciitis. Hopefully the darkness between the widely-spaced bayou path streetlights was heavy enough to hide the lie on my face.

Without a word he fell in beside me, holding my hand and unable to talk further. He stumbled along. We took a shortcut home. Fifteen minutes later he was no better, so he took his blood pressure: 50% higher than usual, which is borderline high on a good day. That night it was scary high.

I put him in bed with a cold cloth on his forehead and snuggled in beside him. I stroked his face and considered forcing him to go to the emergency room. Eric admitted that his jaw hurt, and his sinuses now hurt, too. (The x-rays of his abscessed tooth had shown that the infection had eaten a hole in his jaw and was marching on to his sinus cavities.) We compromised: if his blood pressure came down significantly in half an hour, he'd contact his endodontist, let him know of the worsening situation, ask for a different antibiotic, and enlist his help in moving the oral surgery sooner. His pressure came down just enough that he made it through the night.

The next morning Eric said he felt passable, and promised to call the endodontist first thing, but I knew he wouldn't. I contacted his primary care physician, none other than my father. Dr. Dad suggested in strong terms that I make it clear to the oral surgeon the time had come to do something.

I pinged Eric.

"Too busy," he said, snappish.

"Give me the number."

"Don't have it."

"Give me the name."

He complied, and gave me a list of days he couldn't go. Then he caved. "I'll go today if they can get me in."

I love him. I understood him. I was scared, too.

The endodontist's office responded beautifully, despite my fear that they would dismiss a hysterical wife. Maybe the tremor in my voice as I explained my fears about my husband's general health and heart condition helped. They paged the oral surgeon to let her know that it was an emergency, and the surgeon's assistant moved the procedure up to four days later. Progress.

The assistant interrupted my gushing thank yous to say, "Hold please, it's the surgeon again."

I held for mere seconds.

"Can he go right now? They looked at his films, and the surgeon is clearing her schedule for him. But he has to go now."

"I'll get him there." I left out the "if I have to drag his bloody carcass behind me on a travois" part, but it was implied.

And that is how it came to pass that my husband—who finally accepted that he should worry and obey—ended up with a swollen face and jaw packed with bovine bone three hours later. Thank God for that hyper-responsive surgeon. The culprit for months of undisclosed pain and illness? A hairline crack in his tooth that was too tight to appear on x-rays, but formed a perfect superhighway for bacteria into his jaw tissue.

"Well?" I asked as I bustled him back out to the car.

Through a mouthful of gauze, Eric conveyed in the strongest possible terms that he never wanted to hear his jaw bone scraped again. (Why he chose to remain awake is a mystery to me.) The doctor told him she was optimistic that she had removed all the infected tissue, and that her topical antibiotic was strong enough to deal with what was left behind, but she also kept Eric on oral antibiotics. He was by turns jubilant and chastened, relieved and grateful.

"I ahmrave ahrmto ahrmgo ahrmback," he said. Or tried to.

Translation: besides a normal follow-up about the infection and wound site, he'd been ordered to get another round of bone grafts in January, a metal plate in April, and a new tooth installed the next summer. Plus the follow-up with his cardiologist ASAP. Worse things have happened to nice people, I know, but he was bummed.

Yet in the midst of all this noise was love. Me. The kids. His parents. *Me.*

When we married, Eric had said his greatest goal for our new life was peace. Mind you, he had an overflowing extra-large Samsonite rolling case full of goals that weighed against the possibility of him ever finding it, but what he longed for, now that he had love, was a strife-free zone. A center. A stillness. A safe place to curl up by the fire, legs stretched out, head back, hot chocolate with homemade whipped cream on top in hand. I had promised to give him that. Yeah, me. The one who is a bit, well, mercurial.

But life doesn't allow for perfect peace. You have to find your peace amidst the unceasing chaos of bills, illnesses, injuries, work, heartbreaks, and crises. Eric had lost his peace. He had just flat out lost it. I had failed to give it to him, too. From where he stood, that day was yet another in the latest long list of examples of peace escaping him.

And I understood. I didn't know how to fix it, just like I didn't know for sure how to fix his tooth, or even how to make him stop running, but I was trying. I wanted to figure it out, and I wanted to help him find that chimera, that life without turmoil. Or at least find peace within it. So I ran out while he was in surgery and gathered up a few gifts, hoping they would be the electric paddles that would shock his heart into accepting peace in the here and now.

We got into our crusty old Suburban and Eric opened the gifts. And maybe it was the drugs, maybe it was his jacked-up emotions, but his tears rolled. I helped him put the very manly leather necklace on, to nestle the tiny *E*, *Peace*, and *P* into his thirteen chest hairs against his gigantic heart. It hung out of sight under his shirt, warmed by his skin. I'd waited six years to do this — to replace the gold chain he'd worn since childhood, but that I hated because it was a reminder of the pasts without each other that we had agreed to leave behind.

He held the heavy distressed wooden block with the word "Peace" on it that I hoped he would put in his office, and he read aloud the card that anchored the two gifts:

Peace. It does not mean to be in a place where there is no noise, trouble, or hard work. It means to be in the midst of those things and still be calm in your heart.

I love this card more than I can express. Eric seemed to, too. And that moment felt like the safest time to confess my subterfuge on the previous night, when I had stopped his run. He groaned.

{E-Peace-P}

"I promise to use my powers only for good, never for evil," I said. "But I love you, and hear me loud and clear on this: I won't let you harm yourself."

His nod was barely perceptible, but he did nod.

WRONG TIME ZONE

When Eric lost his father to a long struggle with diabetes, I was in jolly old England, six hours ahead of the time zone my heart prefers to keep. I'd make it home in the nick of time for the funeral, which meant spending those first five days away from Eric when he needed me.

I felt like a cretin, but I knew Eric would have killed me if I'd backed out of my obligation in England. And do you know what the man went and did?

He sent flowers to my chi-chi London hotel. That's right. He worried about me worrying about him, so he sent me a sussie. Now I felt guilty for that, too, but in the best, most grateful, pinch-me-he's-a-dream way. How does he do that?

The flowers were entertaining, too. The front desk woke me up from my post-red-eye snooze to ask if it was OK for them to bring a little surprise up to me. That's the kind of wake-up call I like.

The card was addressed to Mrs. Hutchins. The inside read "From Mr. Hutchins." This is the proper British way of saying "I love you, you sexy creature, from Eric." The British are probably the ones that made Mary Tyler Moore and Dick Van Dyke pretend they slept in separate twin beds on the Dick Van Dyke Show, too.

I loved it. I loved the flowers. I loved my husband. I would love seeing his face when I arrived, tired and worried on Friday night. And I really hated not being there for him. It made it hard to enjoy my first visit to London, which was still pretty awesome, just a lot less awesome than it would have been for us to experience together, and reduced by a factor of ten because we'd lost Larry.

Which is how I know this truth: the greater your need to be home, the harder it will be to get there.

FROM HERE TO ETERNITY

At this point in my career, I should know that I should just stay home. In Houston. With Eric and the kids. But recently I said yes to a day trip to Chicago. BIG mistake.

The first sign of trouble was that in order to make the gig, I had to abandon Eric in Denver, where we were visiting his youngest/our middle child at her college for the weekend. We pulled into our economy motel in Denver at 11:00 Sunday night. Cheap makes me happy, and we got it for a super price, only $49, but cheap didn't include a blow drier this time, I hadn't brought one, and my flight was at seven a.m. Everything else was super, except that we forgot to buy drinks and food, and there was no cheery breakfast buffet or even a basket of fruit when we left at 4:30 the next morning.

I had Google Mapped our directions to the rental car return the night before, but sadly, Google failed us. We followed its directions only to end up at a Holiday Inn five miles from the highway.

The clock was ticking like a wacked-out metronome. We raced back to the highway while I frantically re-Googled, to no avail. We came upon signs to the rental car return. Hallelujah.

We drove up to a locked gate and a sign that advised us after-hours customers to stash the car in long-term parking, then visit their location inside the airport to leave the keys in the drop box. SHIIIITTTTTTT.

We sped to the airport and parked in one of the few and hard-to-find spots. We hopped a bus—of course we were its first stop. It lurched to a stop seven more times before it finally dropped us at the terminal, only three hundred yards from where we'd parked. OMG.

We sprinted to drop our bags—that at least went well—and went on the hunt for the rental car kiosk. It was nearly time for me to board my plane. And in case you forgot, I had really bad hair. We found the kiosk, made the drop, and ratcheted back up to a run for security. We queued up in a ginormous line and watched the big hand move around the watch dial.

As soon as we got in line, our TSA agent struck up a lengthy conversation with the three small children ahead of us. Time dragged. The two TSA agents in the line next to us were spitting people out like a ball thrower, but ours coaxed us through like an old lady in a walker.

When we finally (finally!) made it through, of course we picked the slowest line for the scans. Then we started our dash for the train to get us to our terminal. By this time, my flight was nearly boarded. Eric and I smooched and I took off down one hall while he ran down another for our flights to separate cities. I was the last person to board, but I made it. PHEW.

When I arrived in Chicago refortified from the big breakfast served on the plane (not), the skies were blue and the air crisp. It was going to be a perfect day after all. Really. Until I got in the taxi for the forty-five-minute drive to Naperville. My cabbie either had absolutely no eye-foot coordination or he wanted me to puke. Either way, I spent half the drive with the window down and my head out, gulping in cool air. This had no impact on his driving style or my hair, which still sucked. He managed to get lost, which extended our drive time by ten minutes. We added another five for the flock of Canadian geese crossing the exit ramp that had backed up traffic for a mile.

I made it to my client with all the fat trimmed out of my schedule, and as usual, the minutes leading up to the presentation were tech hell. Not because of my equipment, but because of theirs and their IT person, who literally moved me aside from my laptop to mess with my settings. Never mind I already had it working perfectly. She critiqued my system down to my power cord, slammed my screen when she got frustrated, and ultimately achieved her goal of messing all my shit up. It was five minutes until go time when I forcibly reclaimed it, reset it, and dismissed her in what I hope was a friendly and appreciative manner.

But the presentation was fabulous. No one even mentioned my hair.

Then it was grab a cookie from the trainees' leftovers, repack my gear, retaxi, and retramp to a flight. All of that went fine. I even managed to contact Eric, who was flying out to Tulsa for a few days at about the time I was departing Chicago back to Houston. He had a huge surprise for me:

Eric texted me this picture and "Surprise!"

He had risked missing his flight to retrieve our one-eyed Boston Terrier puppy Petey from boarding at the vet, knowing I would get in that night after the vet closed and have to spend the night sans Eric and sans my Petey Sweetie. Ahhhhhhhhh, I love this man.

But the airlines had a bigger surprise for him. His flight was delayed four hours. Only they couldn't guarantee the delay, and they told him he needed to stay at the airport (rather than return to his office) in case his flight was able to depart earlier.

"Time to turn off and stow away all electronic devices," a disembodied voice announced on my flight. We texted our goodbyes, and I closed my eyes for a nap. When I awoke, we were descending into Houston. I turned on my phone when we were on the runway and texted Eric.

"Run to gate 46. I'm still here, but we're boarding soon," he replied.

A stupid smile cracked my lips. I tucked my bags into a streamlined position, deplaned, and did an OJ through the terminal at Houston Hobby airport.[20]

I huffed and puffed my way to Gate 46. There was a man with a stupid smile to match my own, looking really good in his *Loving the Bike* T-shirt and jeans. I dropped my bags and barreled into him for our bonus hug.

"How long do we have?" I asked against his neck.

"Five minutes," he said and kissed the top of my head.

I remembered the woman who had asked if we were newlyweds on our way out of Houston three days and many cities before. If she could see us now. We might not have the sand and surf, but Burt Lancaster and Deborah Kerr had nothing on us. Five

---

[20] That's an OJ as in running for your flight, not an OJ as in "If the gloves don't fit, you must acquit."

minutes passed in a blink, and then I was waving goodbye as he boarded.

A whirlwind. A frickin frackin hackin schmackin whirlwind. Like our whole lives. I stood there long after the plane pulled away, savoring every beautiful second of my second chance.

HAPPILY EVER AFTER

So that's it: all the secrets I know on how nauseating couples chase the fairy tale. It's a shockingly simple formula, but not an easy one.

Here are the rules:

<u>See It.</u> Look for the best in your partner, your life, and your future. Don't let anything blur your vision. If something blocks your view, move it out of the way. Capture it in an ROA, or something like it. Hold on tight to the positive, to your dream.

<u>Say It.</u> Create your own reality by how you talk about (and to) your loved ones. Shout "He is my hero!" from the highest mountaintops, or on Twitter, even. Make your partner believe in your vision of him and your relationship.

<u>Honor It</u>. Respect that which is important to him. Cheer him (and his football team) on. Participate in some way, even if it's carrying the water bottles. Give up alcohol in support of your teetotaling spouse. Put on your boogie shoes and boot scoot. Make his life bigger, not smaller. Include his dreams in making the vision a reality.

<u>Do It</u>. Old or young, healthy or not, refuse to let the romance die. Woo her, date her. Gaze into her eyes. Touch her, even if only through Skype. Remain physically intimate and sexually together, doing what they do on the Animal Planet, for thirty days and a lifetime.

<u>Be It</u>. Choose. Just choose, no matter what, to hold onto it and to each other. Stop the Whack-a-Mole. Drop the crack baby. Find your peace. Circle back to *See It* and your shared values. Apologize, forgive, forget, and believe.

If this is not your first try at forever, recognize that the odds are stacked higher against you this time, and leave nothing to chance. You're not just fighting against the normal relationship killers— incompatibility, lack of emotional intimacy and support, sexual problems, abuse, and finances; you're now adding in stepparenting, ex-spouses, child support, alimony, meddling smartphones, and how much easier it is to contemplate divorce after you've survived it once. You don't have the luxury of ignoring what you contributed to the failure of your previous relationships. The best predictor of future behavior is past behavior, so identify your poisonous behaviors of the past and choose to behave differently as you move forward. Remember, you may not be marrying the same A-hole you did the first time, but you're bringing the same A-hole with you into your new relationship.

Have I left anything out? Oh, one little thing.

Love. Big love. If you want a relationship that makes your friends queasy, it starts with the one person you can't imagine life without. Don't settle — don't commit with reservation. Find the big love, then spend the rest of your life working to make it even bigger, living happily and imperfectly ever after.

And making everyone else around you want to puke.

DESPITE OUR BEST EFFORTS

It's not that we didn't try to screw this parenting thing up. By all rights, we should have. We did everything that we possibly could that we weren't supposed to do. We gave them refined sugar when they were babies, didn't enforce nap times, spoiled them with expensive and unnecessary gifts. We said yes when we should have said no. We said no when we should have said yes. Our swear jar was always full.

Oh, yeah. And we were one of those "blended families" — you know the kind, the ones with broken homes, divorces, stepparents and complex custody arrangements. Those people. The ones other parents are leery of, like divorce is a communicable disease or something. Who knows? Maybe it is. My own parents even told me once that I had made my children a statistic by choosing to divorce their father. That I had created an at-risk home environment for them.

Me? Perpetual overachiever, business owner, attorney, former cheerleader and high school beauty queen? The one who's never even smoked a cigarette, much less done drugs? My husband? Well, he's the more likely candidate for an at-risk homemaker. Surfer, bass player, triathlon enthusiast. Oh yeah, and chemical engineer and former officer of a ten-billion-dollar company—but you know how those rock-n-rollers are. We probably teeter somewhere between the Bundys and the Cleavers.

But there we were, watching yet another of our kids cross yet another stage for yet another diploma, with honors, with accolades, with activities—with college scholarships, no less. Yeah, I know, yadda yadda yap. There we were, cheering as the announcer called Liz's name. Three of her four siblings rose to clap, too. The fourth one, Thomas, couldn't make it because he was doing time in the state penitentiary in Florida. (Just kidding. He had to work. At a job. That paid him and provided benefits.)

We tried our best to screw it up. We had the perfect formula. But we didn't—not even close. Somehow two losers at their respective Round Ones in love and family unity got it close to perfect on Round Two. By our standards, anyway. Because we didn't give a good goldarnit about anyone else's.

What's more? We got it right on purpose. We made a plan, and we executed the plan. And it worked. After all that effort to screw things up, after the people in our lives who loved us most wrung their hands and whispered behind our backs (and those who didn't love us chortled in anticipation of our certain failure), we went out and done good.

Now, I'm no expert on child rearing (although I've had lots of practice), but I am an expert in helping grownups play nice and behave at work. How annoying is that? I know. I'm a scary hybrid of employment attorney and human resources professional, blended together to create a problem-solving HR consultant. And from where I sat, our blended household—or blendered family, as we call it—looked a lot like a dysfunctional workplace in our early days.

Or a little warren of guinea pigs on which I could conduct my own version of animal testing.

The HR principles I applied at work were, in theory, principles for humans, humans anywhere. Blendering occurs in workplaces when a leadership team gets a couple of new members, and it happens in a home with kids from different families of origins. HR principles = people principles = *blendering* principles. Right? That was my theory, anyway.

Statistics tell me that you, dear reader, are or will be in similar straits: divorced, starting over, trying to make it work. If you've already been there and done that, I hope you've disappointed all your naysayers, too. You'll enjoy this book all the more as you relate to the pains and the joys of blended families. But if you're on the cusp of what feels like an express train descending into hell and wondering how to buy a ticket back, I can help you.

Really.

Okay, probably.

If not probably, then quite possibly.

At the very least, maybe I can say I warned you, or made you laugh. It's a crazy and unpredictable ride, but the destination is worth it.

HOW DID THE BRADYS DO IT?

Blendering Principle #1: It's hard to get anywhere if you don't know where you're going.

Most of the members of my generation know all we need to know about blended families from the Brady Bunch, right?

Not.

Please, folks. That was just a sappy television show, and didn't Florence Henderson have an affair IRL[21] with one of the TV sons? Sounds a lot like incest to me. We clearly need a new set of role models, yet I'd be vacationing in Fiji right now if I had a nickel for every time someone said to me, "Oh! You're just like the Brady Bunch!"

---

[21] In real life.

The Bradys wove their magic through engaging scripts and clever sets, cute young actors and the star power of Florence Henderson. Eric and I didn't have those crutches to lean on. Neither will you.

Real blended families start with two adults who want to pledge their troth, which in English means they want to marry. Or at least cohabitate with commitment. Oh, hell, maybe not even that. But that conundrum brings us to the genesis of our blended family success, and IMHO[22], a critical element.

Each of our kids had already endured one familial breakup. Were we ready to provide them stability and an example of enduring love? If not, why would we knowingly put them through sure trauma again? Nothing is certain in life, but Eric and I were all in. Not only were we all in, but we both had a consuming desire to demonstrate to our children the type of relationship we dreamed of for them, and neither of us felt like we had done so in our past lives. Scratch that. We absolutely *knew* we had not done so in our past lives.

So, we were madly in love and promised forever. Believed forever. Were confident in forever.

---

[22] In my humble opinion. Seriously, folks, get with the pop culture.

Still, this left a lot up to chance.

Pretend for a second that you married a touchy-feely HR consultant. Imagine that she had a penchant for things like mission, vision, and values statements. Picture her love of goal-setting and accountability. Some of you have mentally drawn up your divorce papers already.

Eric didn't. He and I created a relationship operating agreement (ROA) for ourselves as a couple. I may or may not have promised years of sexual favors to secure his participation, but his attitude about the project was good. Now, this isn't a relationship book. Well, it is, in a way. It is a book about our relationships with our children within a blended family. But it is not a couples' relationship book, so I'll spare you the gory details behind the ROA.

While we entered into our ROA to make our great relationship stronger, we did so knowing it would set the framework for co-parenting. Why? Because our kids were the most important things to each of us, besides one another. And since most second marriages break down over issues of stepparenting, money, or sex. Hell, many first marriages crash and burn on those issues. We had less than ideal co-parenting relationships with our exes, for sure.

So here's how our ROA looks:

Our (Exceptionally Wonderful) Marriage
Mantra: Make it all small stuff.

Our relationship's purpose is to create a loving, nurturing, safe environment that enables us to
- make a positive, joyful difference in each other's lives,
- respect each other's needs and differences,
- encourage each other's spiritual, emotional, and physical needs and development,
- practice caring, open communication,
- role-model loving relationships to our children, and
- work as partners when we parent and make major decisions.

Because we recognize that life is not always about the incredible highs, we are committed to these strategies:
- Stop, breathe, and be calm.
- Allow ourselves to cherish and be cherished.
- Be positive. Assume a positive intent and give a positive response. Speak your mind as positively as possible.

- Be reasonable. Am I being oversensitive? Am I dragging my own issues in unnecessarily?
- Be considerate. Is there anything to gain from what I am about to say? Is this the right time to say it?
- Be respectful. Don't mope, don't name-call, don't yell, don't be sarcastic.
- Be open. Explain your intent.
- Be present. Don't walk away, physically or emotionally.
- Be aware of time and energy. After 60 minutes, stop talking. Schedule another conversation for 24 hours later if there's no resolution.
- Make it safe to cry "calf rope."
- *Be* it. Do the behaviors you're seeking in each other within an hour of the first conversation.
- Be loving. Don't go to bed angry or with things unresolved.

He asks of her:
- Trust and have faith that I love you, enough that we don't have to solve everything the second it happens.
- Assume a positive intent.
- Listen, don't interrupt.

- Don't be sarcastic.

She asks of him:
- Come back to me faster and don't drag things out, because I need you.
- Speak your mind assertively, and don't be sarcastic.
- Don't assume the actions I take are always because of you.
- Assume a positive intent.

We didn't get this smart on our own. Both of us were trained to draft this type of agreement in our work lives, one of us more than the other. I specialize in working with hyper-competitive, confident-bordering-on-egomaniacal executives who are somewhat lacking in people skills, so I've spent years mediating, soothing, recalibrating, and at times walloping high-level business people into line. One of the best tools to get all the warring co-workers from different backgrounds to reach détente is an operating agreement. Even better? An operating agreement grounded in shared values, vision, and mission.

This worked so well for me with one of my problem executives that we ended up married. In fact, you just read our operating agreement.

Blendering Principle #2: Your mom was almost right: Do unto others as *they* would have done unto them.

So we addressed parenting, but more importantly, we addressed how we would handle ourselves in situations of higher stress and greater conflict. All of our commitments about behavior applied equally to the parenting context. Now, when a parent/stepparent decision point arose, we could act in accordance with pre-agreed principles.

Or we could try.

Execution got a little sloppy at times. When it did, we always had the agreement to return to, a touchstone, a refocusing point, a document which reminded us that for all we didn't agree on, there was oh-so-much-more that we did.

We filtered our day-to-day co-parenting decisions through this model. Chores, allowances, length of skirts, cell phones—you name it, we used it. Even better, we used it when we designed our family structure and plan. Did I mention I believe in planning? I believe in plans. And I believe in modifying the plan within the context of agreed principles when new circumstances arise. We got the chance for a lot of planning and re-planning, right from the start.

When Eric and I first married, his eldest son Thomas had graduated from college and had a real job, Eric's middle daughter Marie was entering college in the South, and his youngest daughter Liz lived with her mother on the East Coast. My Susanne was in elementary school, and my ADHD son Clark was in middle school; they split their time between their father and me. Our original parenting plan called for the two youngest kids to live mostly with us, for Liz to visit frequently, and for us to see Marie and Thomas as often as possible.

We envisioned all of our children, and someday their children, in our home as frequently as we could get them there. We bought a house in a great school district in Houston, with a veritable dormitory of four bedrooms upstairs and our master bedroom on the far side of the downstairs—because we love our kids even more from a distance. And how could we resist this house? It has a lush back yard with a three-level pond full of fat goldfish and koi that reminds us of the home we left behind on St. Croix in the U.S. Virgin Islands.

Just as this is not a book about couples' relationships, it is also not a book about divorce or custody battles. I could dish on those, but I won't, because even though I've changed the names of all parties in this little tome to protect the innocent[23], some things should and will remain private. They were painful. Isn't that the case in all divorces? You don't divorce because the relationship exceeded your expectations. You don't divvy up with a light heart the time you will spend with children you cherish. Most of you don't, anyway, and we sure didn't.

So, for whatever reason, within four months of "I do," Liz had taken up primary residence with us in Texas, and a year later Marie transferred to a university two hours away. I had never pictured myself taking a role of such primacy with two teenage stepdaughters. Teenage girls get a bad rap for good reason. It's not the easiest time in their lives, or the easiest time for the people that love them, even with great girls like Liz and Marie. Yet this new arrangement fit the model we envisioned. We just needed to flex. A lot.

---

[23] Criteria that requires Eric and me to use our real names.

I held onto my husband's hand for dear life and sucked in one deep, cleansing breath after another. We could do this. I could do this. We would have no regrets or remorse, we would give our kids the best we could, and be damn happy doing it. Yeah!

And so, very carefully and very cautiously, we began to blender.

BLENDERING

Blendering Principle #3: Culture is everything.

Family culture evolves slowly, but it eventually becomes so ingrained that even though most of the time we take it for granted, we will go to battle over it in a heartbeat.

And at our house, sometimes we do. It is who we are. We're a feisty group, in a good way. Call it self-confidence. So, what happens when who we are — the family structure we've always had — changes? What survives, what dies, and what is reborn? Our kids had a lot of good stuff they wanted to hang on to: summer vacations in Maine for his kids, Christmas in New Mexico for mine, Thanksgiving dinner menus, birthday breakfasts of half-baked chocolate chip pancakes for his girls, rabid devotion to Texas A&M football in my house.

Eric and I faced a restructuring challenge when his then-thirteen-year-old daughter Liz moved in with us, Clark (11) and Susanne (9). We had navigated the "stepsiblings living in separate houses" issue before, and while that was not without its perils, the boats had sailed on relatively smooth waters. Our main issue until the blender event was hurt feelings over time each parent spent with non-birth kids.

And then we blendered. With that plan I mentioned earlier. And a schedule. Preceded by research. (My poor husband, I know.) But what we wanted to co-create was too important to leave to chance.

We had just moved to Houston from the Caribbean, so we found ourselves with three friendless kids newly thrown together in the house for a long summer of empty days with only me—I work from home—to shepherd them. Oh yeah, and we were broke. Zero cash, flat-out broke. We weren't going to be able to throw expensive days at Schlitterbahn Water Park at this problem.

Our plan involved holding themed family events on the cheap each night of the week. Monday, ping-pong. Tuesday, board games. Wednesday, movies. Thursday, kids cook. Friday, swim night. Saturday, family night out (on a strict budget).

We had a rotation for which kid got to choose the details; which movie, which board game, the menu, what our night out would be. We kept up this schedule all summer and some vestiges remain, years later.

It was powerfully effective. Why?

Because everything we did, we did as a family. And we made memories. We did not sit around and whine about what to do; we were active. We established a pattern that the kids looked forward to repeating. We honored each other's choices, even when we hated them. Although we weren't above bartering with Clark to try to get out of another game of Risk on game night.

Now, this blender summer was not without tears. It wasn't without tense moments, angry Facebook statuses (woopsie), and one-on-one conversations between parent and child. We expected that. It was okay. We had kids with big emotions that we were trying to move from fear and hurt into love and faith. Each of the kids worked with a counselor at various points in the process, to mixed but generally positive results. We found a great church where Liz made friends and joined the choir.

And we gently evolved those one-on-one parent-child conversations into parent-parent-child as the weeks went on. We partnered, as we had agreed. It was uncomfortable at times. But we were becoming *real*. Like a family. So we kept up with the plan.

We did other bonding silliness. At the end of the summer, we paid for dinner for five at P.F. Chang's with the parental contributions to the $1 swear jar. I told my kids they should thank me for finding a stepfather whose colorful language paid off so well. We paid for one month's water bill with the kids' deposits into the $1 turn-off-the-lights jar. We doled out chores on a rotating schedule because nobody wanted to clean up dog poop three weeks in a row during the Houston summer. We enacted a strict oldest-to-youngest rule to avoid constant battles and fears of favoritism, like who got to ride shotgun. Poor Susanne never got to sit in the front seat. She's still claiming abuse.

Another tradition we kicked off that first summer was picking up tacky souvenirs when we traveled. Not just any old tacky souvenirs, but odd, gaudy and large objects that received a place of honor in our living room display. We made our first purchase the day before our wedding; we bought a jeweled wire gecko—a hideously beautiful creature. On a weekend trip to Brenham, Texas, in July of that first summer, the kids added Lenny, a wood and tin armadillo. This tradition thrives still. Our family treasures include a steel cowboy, a log grizzly bear, a ceramic dancing hula cat, and many more gauche objets d'art.

By August, we decided our fledgling relationships were ready to leave the nest; we attempted a two-week migration from Houston to Maine and back with the five of us in the Suburban. The destination was key. As the latest comer into the blended household, we wanted Liz to have the opportunity to introduce her new siblings to a special Hutchins place. Some of her best memories were from her grandparents' cabin on Lake Mooselookmeguntic.

So Maine it would be.

ABOUT THE AUTHOR

Pamela Fagan Hutchins lives, loves, laughs, works, and writes in Texas with her husband Eric and their blended family of three dogs, one cat, and the youngest few of their five offspring. She is the award winning author of many books, including *The Clark Kent Chronicles, How To Screw Up Your Kids, Love Gone Viral, Hot Flashes And Half Ironmans, Puppalicious And Beyond, Saving Grace* and a contributing author to *Prevent Workplace Harassment, Ghosts!, Easy To Love But Hard To Raise,* and *Easy To Love But Hard To Teach.*

Pamela is an employment attorney and human resources professional, and the co-founder of a human resources consulting company. She spends her free time hiking, running, bicycling, and enjoying the great outdoors.

For more information, visit http://pamelahutchins.com, or email her at pamela@pamelahutchins.com. To receive her e-newsletter for announcements about new releases, click on http://eepurl.com/iITR.

SkipJack Publishing:
http://SkipJackPublishing.com/

CPSIA information can be obtained at www.ICGtesting.com
Printed in the USA
LVOW130554031012

301142LV00001B/3/P